INDIAN STORIES
from the
PUEBLOS

INDIAN STORIES
FROM THE
PUEBLOS

By

FRANK G. APPLEGATE

FOREWORD BY
Witter Bynner

ILLUSTRATIONS FROM
ORIGINAL PUEBLO
INDIAN PAINTINGS

APPLEWOOD BOOKS

BEDFORD, MASSACHUSETTS

1994

Indian Stories from the Pueblos was first published by Lippincott in 1929.

ISBN 1-55709-227-3

Front cover: *Pueblo Dwellings* by Maxfield Parrish.

Thank you for purchasing an Applewood Book. Applewood Books reprints America's lively classics—books from the past that are still of interest to modern readers. For a free copy of our catalog, please write to Applewood Books, 18 North Road, Bedford, MA 01730.

10 9 8 7 6 5 4 3 2 1

Library of Congress Cataloging-in-Publication Data:
Applegate, Frank G. (Frank Guy), 1882-1931.
    Indian stories from the Pueblos / by Frank G. Applegate.
        p.   cm.
    Originally published: Philadelphia: Lippincott, 1929.
    ISBN 1-55709-227-3
    1. Pueblo Indians—Legends.   2. Hopi Indians—
        Legends.   I. Title.
E99.P9A64   1994
398.2'089'974—dc20   93—47398

Publisher's Note

No program of American books would be complete without the remarkable documents of the intrusion of European America on Native America. Unfortunately, there are very few written examples of Native American primary sources available today. However, during the nineteenth and early twentieth centuries, a popular interest in "Indians" brought forth a large number of books by "non-Indians," some of whom actually lived among the Nations and tried objectively to document tribal life. The best of these books now reveal a wealth of information on Native American life, customs, and folk-lore, and expose the popular cultural view of Native Americans by those from the outside. These texts turn into both a timeline of social progress in America and informative and loving books on the subjects they honor. Because of the place in time of these books, sometimes reading their texts may make a modern reader, especially one with a sophisticated degree of familiarity with the history, take exception. However, we believe they are nonetheless informative and entertaining, as long as they are taken in the context of their time.

Indian Stories from the Pueblos was originally published in 1929. The book is a combination of tales and legends of Early Pueblo days and stories told to the author, Frank Applegate, while he lived among the Pueblos.

Mr. Applegate was born in Illinois in 1882.

Shortly after 1920, he moved to Santa Fe. As a painter and an author, Frank Applegate became a leader among the artists and writers who were drawn to New Mexico at that time. He also found sympathy with the Pueblo people around him, and he became a familiar face among the Hopi.

A recent reading of the book by Joe S. Sando, a Pueblo and the foremost authority on Pueblo life, has pointed out some of the aspects of the book which he believes are in error. He believes that many of the stories are corrupted historical events of New Mexico and has listed the following factual errors. On page 6, "cacique" is a Taino Indian word from the Caribbean, they spoke the Arowak language. In the chapter "The Snake Priest's Trousers" and again in "Cochiti Ancient Hunting Dance," it is the moieties, or kiva members, who perform the dances; a "clan" is a blood line coming from a common grandmother, or cognates. On page 43, skunk skin around the ankles is for decoration, not to prevent evil. On page 46, the Pueblos continue to appeal or pray both ways. On page 47, San Ysidro is carried throughout the fields on May 15 by both the Pueblo Indians and the Spanish of New Mexico. On page 68, Indians do not beat on hollow logs. On page 79, the rattle is usually carried in the right hand. On page 82, the place is usually called Yungue Oweengue. On page 87, one needs a bowl or tub to whip the amole into a lather to wash the hair. On page 95, Indians also use holy water. On page 101, Indians use the sun as years and moon as months; two suns equal two years and one moon equals one month in European language. On page 109, the Hopi-Tewa of Hano escaped to Arizona during the third revolt in 1696. On page 122, serpent or snake clan is possible, but still it is the society that performs the snake dance. On page 138, Comanches did not arrive in the Southwest until 1704, so the raiders had to be Apaches, who arrived sometime after 1400. On page 146, Apaches not Comanches. On page 147, not Sandia, but at a place called Kuaau and known as Coronado Monument today. On page 152, survivors did not reach New Mexico, but crossed the Rio Grande in the Big Bend country of Texas and into Northern Mexico. Page 171, this could be Pose Oweengue, not Pose uingge. Oweengue means village in Tewa.

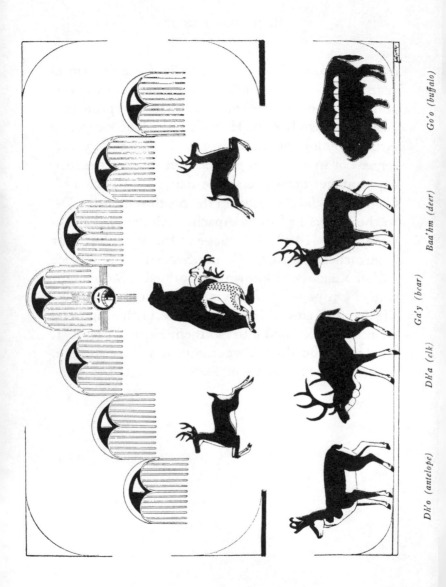

Dk'o (antelope)   Dk'a (elk)   Ga'y (bear)   Baa'hm (deer)   Go'o (buffalo)

INDIAN GAME ANIMALS

In this picture the important game animals of the Pueblo Indians are shown, all of which they formerly hunted. The Tewa Pueblo Indian names of these animals are Go'o (buffalo), Baa'hn (deer), Dh'o (antelope), Dh'a (elk), and Ga'y (bear).
At the top of the picture is the sun surrounded by rain-bearing clouds.

INDIAN STORIES
FROM THE
PUEBLOS

By

FRANK G. APPLEGATE

FOREWORD BY
Witter Bynner

ILLUSTRATIONS FROM
ORIGINAL PUEBLO
INDIAN PAINTINGS

J. B. LIPPINCOTT COMPANY

PHILADELPHIA & LONDON

1929

PREFACE

In the parts of this book where Indians have told their own stories, some terms are used by them that are not Pueblo Indian in origin, but are those introduced by whites in trying to explain Indian religious beliefs and now used by some of the Indians themselves in attempting to re-explain their beliefs to the whites.

Only the cacique or high priest of a pueblo has a complete understanding of the religious beliefs of his village, and he imparts this knowledge only to his acolytes, one of whom is to succeed him when he dies. The majority of the Pueblo Indians thus have little knowledge of the inner meaning of their religion and of the ceremonies they perform. No white person has yet adequately explained Pueblo Indian religious beliefs, although many have described well certain phases of their beliefs and rituals.

The Pueblo Indians have no belief in an anthropomorphic supreme being, nor even in a great spirit, such as is ascribed to them by some careless writers. In its purest form their religion is a belief that cosmic spirit permeates the whole universe, so that everything, even inanimate objects, contain some of this cosmic spirit. By prayers, incantations, and ceremonies they believe that some of this cosmic spirit—or spirits drawn from the cosmic spirit— may be influenced for their benefit, and they also believe that in the sun and earth reside great sources of creative cosmic spirit that they can call forth and use for their own purposes; and that from these sources evil forces also can be released by incantation for evil by those so minded. These prayers are considered by them black, and their use is strictly forbidden by pueblo law, and anyone so using them is severely punished as a wizard.

In each pueblo there are societies or organizations for performing the religious rituals for the benefit of the pueblo as a whole. The priests, who are the heads of these societies, and even the cacique, are erroneously called medicine men by some people, though this term can be applied properly only to the shamans of the hunting tribes.

There are six distinct languages spoken among the Pueblo Indians mentioned in this book, and religious practices vary considerably between those pueblos where one language is spoken and those where an entirely different language is used. Because of there being so many different languages there are some terms used in pueblo nomenclature taken from one of the pueblo languages or from the Spanish and now understood by all the pueblos. Examples of this are: cacique, a Mexican word; koshare, a Keres term; kiva, a Hopi term, etc., etc.

There are many different forms of the matachina dance given by Indians all the way from Taos in northern New Mexico to lower Old Mexico two thousand miles distant. Some of these dances are still almost pagan while some show strong influence of Christian missionary teaching. Also there are a great many versions of the Montezuma legend both in New Mexico and Old Mexico. This legend in many places has likewise been much influenced by the teachings of Christianity.

FRANK G. APPLEGATE

Foreword

Whether these tales Mr. Applegate brings us from the Pueblo Indians of the Southwest relate to their early history or to their present-day doings and feelings, to the early history of Spaniards among them or to the intrusion of later comers from the white world, the substance of most of them and the telling of all of them make living folk-stories. One who knows Pueblo Indians catches their true accent on page after page of Mr. Applegate's homely and vivid record. Bare as the style is, it exerts a spell like the bareness of Indians in one of their apparently simple dance-rhythms. It is akin to the style of fairy-stories. Much as one used to sit engrossed at a story-teller's knee and listen to accounts of folk in whom children believe, so one listens now to these narratives of child-like faith, devout adventure and humorous encounter on the part of a folk as enchanted in their way as ever was Jack the Giant-Killer or Br'er Rabbit and yet a folk living real lives among us grown-ups in New Mexico and Arizona, to the delight of artists and tourists and to the despair of the Indian Bureau.

One wonders less at Mr. Applegate's ability to make his informal paragraphs seem to be spoken in an Indian voice, when one knows of his intimate and sympathetic life among the Pueblos. Not only is he a familiar in the Tewa villages around his home town, Santa Fe, but months at a time he has lived in Hopi villages, lived the Hopi life, felt Hopi feelings, studied and revived Hopi art among the native pottery-makers, painted Hopi persons and ceremonies and listened meantime to such stories as he has caught for us in this volume. He has caught them as patiently, as gently, as surely, as I have seen an Indian pick up in gifted hands a live wood-pecker from a tree-trunk or a live trout from a stream.

WITTER BYNNER

SANTA FE, NEW MEXICO
May 12, 1929

Contents

Contents

Illustrations

INDIAN STORIES

from the

PUEBLOS

———————

ANCESTRAL EAGLES

Tabo Salukama, Hopi Indian, had, when a small lad, been snatched away from his parents by the Indian Police and sent by the Indian Agent, along with other Hopi boys and girls, hundreds of miles away to an Indian boarding school. At this school he had been kept for eight years without returning once to the pueblo and, during all this time, he had had it impressed upon him that Indians were savages and that their religious practices and ceremonies were the result of low and base superstitions. He was also taught that the middle-class American culture was the flower of highest civilization and that all Americans were one hundred per cent pure in their ideals, religious beliefs and practices. Likewise he was taught that the Indian Bureau and its agents were always solicitous for the welfare of the Indians and always stood ready to help them in any emergency. Tabo came gradually to believe all this, so that when he returned to his sky-high home, his head was full to overflowing with white man's nonsense and he disdained and disapproved all things Indian and was the despair of his parents. Nothing Indian was good enough for him. Hopi religious ceremonies and their worship of "false gods" disgusted him and the eternal odors of stewing mutton and goat's meat sickened him. Corn meal porridge and dried peaches were, to him, no fit sort of substitute for boarding-school rolled oats and stewed prunes. Fortunately the keen air of the high altitude gave Tabo such an overpowering appetite that he soon overcame his repugnance for the hearty Indian food, and a few months later his mother gave him as husband to a nice Hopi girl who had shown herself proficient in the difficult art of grinding corn with the metate or mealing stone.

Tabo was now confronted with the emergency of making a living for himself and wife and he soon found out how profitless was all he had learned while at school. But his father-in-law took him in hand and taught him how to plant his corn and squashes and tend his peach trees, so that they would yield, even in the desert's sandy and thirsty soil. Tabo tried for awhile to live according to the missionary's teachings and prayed fervently every day for his corn and squashes, but when his corn began to turn yellow, in spite of his prayers for rain, he suddenly lost faith in what the Indians call "the Sunday Jesus" and reverted to his ancient and primitive tribal gods and joined the other Hopis in their great rain-making ceremony. Soon afterwards the overdue summer rains arrived and confirmed his reborn faith in the old gods, so that thenceforward he was one with the Hopis in their belief that their own gods are best for them, although Jesus may be able to help the white man.

After this demonstration of the efficacy of the old tribal Katchinas, or Spirits, Tabo took part in all the religious rites and ceremonies of his people, and the death of a maternal uncle a few years later leaving him as chief of his clan, he became a very important figure in Hopi affairs.

Now one of the grandest ceremonies in all the Hopi calendar is the Niman Katchina, or farewell to the gods. These gods, or Katchinas, after dwelling with the Hopis during the spring and early summer, leave for their homes in the far distant San Francisco Mountains, which sparkle like a gem on the distant Hopi horizon and seem a fitting setting for the homes of gods. At dawn on the next day after the Katchinas have gone there is a ceremony by the chiefs of the clans at which each chief dispatches the spirit of a golden eagle that it may hurry to the returned gods with messages to remind them not to neglect sending the proper amount of rain to mature the Hopi corn for the year.

It is very essential that each clan chief have an eagle for this ceremony, so all the country round about Hopiland for fifty miles is carefully mapped out by the Hopis and a section set aside for each clan chief as his eagle hunting ground, on which no one else is to trespass in search of eagles. In the spring each clan chief seeks out the eagle nest in his territory and selects one of its eaglets and brings it to the pueblo, so that it may mature in time for the Niman ceremony.

Now one year when Tabo climbed up the crag where his eagle nest was located he found that some-one had been ahead of him and stolen an eaglet. He was very much incensed at this but was too conservative to jeopardize the supply of eagles of future years by taking another one, so he descended the crag and started searching for the thief. He had not far to go for he soon met up with a Navajo Indian sheep herder who frequented that part of the country, and in whose possession he found the eagle.

When he accused the Navajo of the theft and demanded his eagle, the Navajo only laughed at him and told him, in what was the equivalent in Indian sign language, to go chase himself, that he had found the eagle on his own herding ground, and that it now belonged to him.

The Hopis are a peace-loving people and are re-luctant to employ violence to further their ends, so Tabo left the Navajo and went trustingly straight to the Indian Agent, feeling sure that in this case where the right was so obviously on his side he would be able to procure swift and complete justice. The agent, who was new to the country and its problems, could make neither head nor tail of Tabo's story, but finally to get rid of him he gave Tabo a written order on the Navajo to give over the eagle. Tabo took the order with profuse thanks and trotted confidently back the forty miles to the sheep camp and trustingly handed the paper to the herder. Now this Navajo had not had the advantage of the schooling given Tabo, since, being a nomad in this great desert country, it had been easy for him to evade the Indian Police at the time when he should have gone to school, so he knew nothing of the "paper that talks." But he took the paper from Tabo and looked at it, then reached in his pouch and took out a familiar-looking bag and poured some tobacco from it into the creased paper, then carefully rolled up the paper and tobacco into a small cylinder, and placed one end of it in his mouth, lighted the other end of it with a match and proceeded to smoke it. Tabo looked on this desecration amazed and outraged and expected every moment to see the Navajo struck dead in some mysterious manner, but on nothing of the sort happening, he took courage and again demanded the eagle, whereupon the Navajo drove him from the camp.

Tabo again took his tale of woe to the agent, but the agent was by now bored by the affair, the ins and outs of which he could not comprehend, and had Tabo put out of his office.

Tabo now retired to his home to brood over the wrongs and the injustices of the agent. He finally reasoned that the agent was only a very small and rather ineffectual factor and that his intelligence was hardly adequate to understand the seriousness of the present crisis, in which the future crops and welfare of the Hopis were jeopardized by his incompetency, so Tabo came to the conclusion that the only thing to do was to apprise the chief at Washington of the emergency that was imminent.

The next day Tabo spent in composing and writing the following letter:

Dear Chief of Indian Bureau:
This same has come to pass here. Bad Navajo Indian have get my eagle wich i require for Niman Kachina, So no rain coming maybe for Hopis. Make corn die. Me i tell it to Hopi Indian agent. He say it to me, No require no eagle. Sunday Jesus Katchina send rain when need. i tell to him like hell no, i pray like hell one time with Jesus Katchina. He no send rain and corn get sick. Then i get rain from Hopi Katchina. I don get eagle pretty dam Quick now Hopis maybe got no corn. Navajo got too plenty sheeps no got use for eagles. Please big white chief for Indian, make police get eagle to me from naughty Navajo. i submit myself to your loving care,
Tabo Salukama, Hopi Indian.

This letter a week later landed in the Indian Bureau at Washington and was duly laid on the desk of a young, newly appointed under clerk, who a few weeks before had been a salesman in a cigar store in Philadelphia and whose nearest acquaintance with an Indian, heretofore, had been with the wooden one in front of the building. After studying the letter the clerk read up on various subjects and sent back the following reply:

Mr. Taby Salukama, Dear Sir:

Your communication of recent date has been received and your problems have been given the greatest consideration by the bureau. The bureau is having sent to you under separate cover the following list of bulletins of the Department of Agriculture. #754 Raptores and their control. #1263 Proper Picking of Yellow Dent Seed Corn for Increased Germination. #968 Sheep Dips for Exterminating Ticks. #987 Methods of Dry Farming in Western Kansas. #547 Earth Worms and Their Contributions to Soil Upbuilding.

The Bureau feels assured that these bulletins will solve your difficulties for you. The bureau further suggests that you consult the nearest farm bureau relative to your problems. If, as you suggest, the eagles are carrying off your sheep you should take it up with the agent there and perhaps he can supply you with poisoned grain so that you may rid your pastures of these undesirable birds, or he may be able to procure a government hunter for a short period to shoot them.

Department of the Interior,
Indian Bureau.

Tabo was overjoyed when he received a bulky package and a letter from Washington. He was sure that his troubles would soon be over and he would quickly have his precious eagle in his possession. It was about time too, for the Niman Katchina ceremony was only two weeks distant now. Tabo examined his mail, but not having time to figure out what it was all about, he hastened off to the agent to consult him further about it. The agent looked at the letter and the bulletins and then told Tabo he could go and try them on the Navajo if he liked, but not to bother the Indian Bureau with any more letters or to annoy him further. The truth of the matter was that the agent was reluctant to interfere with the Navajo, for Navajos are only too ready to take their own part when they think their rights are being invaded, while the Hopi is so peace loving that he will allow himself to be imposed upon.

This time when Tabo approached, the Navajo picked up a stone and threw it at him. Tabo was beginning to lose faith in the white man's help now, but he was willing to take one more chance on Washington, so he went home and this time he wrote a letter to the President. As he wrote he felt a resurgence of faith in the white man, for surely the great white father would not permit such rank injustice as had fallen to his lot. The President could even send soldiers to recover his eagle for him. Tabo's letter to the President ran:

Dear sir Precident of U. S.
Please send soldiers to get my eagle from Navajo, talk paper no damn good for Navajo. Niman Katchina coming too soon now. I don get eagle pretty dam quick now Hopis maybe starve for no rain to wet corn. Tell soldiers, look out, Navajo no good, throw stone to me for one time soon.
Please dont wait to hesitate for the present and delay.

Loving,
Tabo Salukama.

The last ten days before the going of the gods, Tabo was in a fever of expectation. He scanned the horizon continually every day watching for the soldiers that were to come to restore his eagle before it should be too late, but on the morning before the Niman Katchina, instead of soldiers, came a letter marked "Office of the President." Tabo hastily tore it open and read:

Mr. Tabo Salukama
Dear Sir:
Your recent letter has been referred to the Indian Bureau and we trust that your claim will be speedily adjusted to your complete satisfaction.

Per ———, Secy.

The Niman ceremonies were over and the greatest of all the Hopi gods had gone back to their ancestral homes in the far away San Francisco Mountains. The next morning at dawn the spirits of the eagles must be released to carry messages to the great Katchina gods of the Hopis to remind them that they must not forget to arrange for plenty of rain for the Hopi cornfields. Tabo had, as a peaceful Indian, done his utmost in every peaceful way to recover his clan eagle, without success, so now his mind began to move in an old and almost obliterated groove. He returned to his home early that day and had his wife prepare a succulent and sustaining stew of mutton and dried peaches. At dusk he dispensed with all his clothing, with the exception of a gee string and moccasins, and covered his body with red ochre paint, with the exception of a few green stripes. Then he took a very old and much worn ancestral club from a niche over a roof beam and faded silently away in the night, as only an Indian can fade, in the direction of a distant and lonely sheep camp far out in the desert.

The next morning at dawn the full quota of eagle spirits was released by the Hopi clan chiefs to carry their messages to the all-powerful Katchinas in the distant San Francisco Mountains, although it might have been observed that one feather was missing from the tail of Tabo's eagle. Just at this moment a distant Navajo sheep herder discovered that the same missing feather was gripped tightly in his hand. The Navajo was recovering from a long spell of unconsciousness, in which he had imagined that he was flying through the air on the back of an eagle at a great height, when suddenly he had fallen to the ground, alighting on his head. Now with one hand he was feeling a great lump above his eyebrow, while with his eyes he was looking intently at the eagle feather, which he was already beginning, superstitiously, to blame for his great fall through the sky.

THE SNAKE PRIEST'S TROUSERS

THE SNAKE PRIEST'S TROUSERS

MOST people entertain the traditional misconception that Indians possess no sense of humor, and think of them as being at all times dignified, solemn-faced, and diffident. As a matter of fact, no people are more easily diverted than those first Americans who dwell in the pueblos of our southwest. But humor is conditioned by a racial point of view, and a situation that a Hopi Indian finds most laughable leaves us bewildered, while one we would find highly amusing would as likely as not cause a Hopi Indian to weep. This I discovered only after several months living with the Hopi Indians in Arizona.

The red letter day of the whole Hopi calendar is that of the ceremonial snake dance, in which the men of the snake clan dance with live rattlesnakes, in the optimistic belief that such an action will insure an abundance of rainfall to mature the growing corn. Now the Hopis may be deluded by their belief in the efficacy of the snake dance for this purpose, but they are nevertheless very earnest in its practice, and in order that there may be plenty of rattlers for the ceremony the members of the whole snake clan hunt for four consecutive days, each day toward a different world quarter, and gather in all the snakes that they find and bring them to the pueblo.

In this hunt the Indians go entirely naked, except for a little paint and exceptionally abbreviated trunks. In their hands they carry a snake bag, a small bag of ceremonial corn meal and an eagle feather attached to the end of a wand, and when one of the Indians finds a rattlesnake he sprinkles it with a little of the sacred meal, strokes it lightly with the eagle feather until it straightens out and then with a lightning-like movement seizes the snake just back of the head and claps it into the snake bag before his snakeship really knows what has happened.

At the going down of the sun the snake clan foregathers at the ceremonial snake kiva, an underground room, to count and dispose of their catch.

The hunts, when I saw them, were led by Súpela, the great snake chief, a man prominent in Hopi affairs. Just as it was growing dark on the last day of one of the hunts, and two days before the snake dance, I was up on the mesa in the pueblo of Walpi talking with a Hopi friend, when suddenly from the highest house-top on the mesa the voice of the official village crier sounded through the pueblo.

Immediately every Indian stopped whatever he

happened to be doing at the moment, and turning in the direction from which the voice came, listened intently, so as not to miss a single syllable of what was being said. The voice would rise to a high and eerie minor and then gradually lower through an octave and then rise again, setting every ear-drum in the pueblo to vibrating and filling all the darkness with the weird and strange cadences.

As the proclamation of the crier ended, every Indian face about me wore a concerned and serious expression, as though the news of a great calamity had just been announced. I immediately concluded that some terrible catastrophe was imminent, or that it had already taken place. It flashed through my mind that perhaps the deadly rattlesnakes had gotten away from the hunters and were even then scattering through the already darkening pueblo, ready to deal death to anyone they might meet. Finally, unable longer to control my concern, I turned to my Hopi friend, who was discussing with bystanders in a lugubrious tone of voice what I had taken to be a near tragedy, and I asked him what the crier had said.

"Well," my friend answered with a troubled and woebegone air, "he say, while the snake chief was out to hunting snakes to-day to make snake dance with, someone, he do not know who, come to snake ceremonial kiva and take his pair of pants which is blue and stole them also, and now Su'pela, the snake chief, he is get very mad and he want his pants back to him very soon, because he wish to go home to his supper, and he say for everyone look out for pants and get them back for him once more very quick, and he also say man who take his pants are very bad man to do so."

Now not a single Hopi saw anything ludicrous whatever about this situation. They were as serious about it as we would be hilarious should Hoover suddenly send radio proclamations over the land, announcing that while he was in his office attending to the affairs of the nation someone had appropriated his pajamas so that he couldn't go to bed, and that he was very angry about it, and for everyone to be on the lookout for them and get them back to him without delay.

But though the Hopis saw nothing humorous in the episode of the snake chief's pants, I saw them become almost hysterical laughing at a perennial farce which is enacted by a group of them each winter, in which the whole humor of the comedy hinges on the point that a Hopi maiden makes a proposal of marriage without first arranging her hair exactly in the customary manner for such an occasion, a thing which went entirely over my head.

Some time after the snake chief had recovered

his denim overalls and the snake dance of that year
had passed into history, I was sitting with him on
one of the far out-jutting rocks of the Walpi mesa
top and we were looking off across the sun-
drenched desert to the south. He was pointing out
prehistoric pueblo ruins of the Hopis and telling
me tales of their peregrinations previous to their
settling on their present inaccessible, rocky mesa,
when I noticed his eye fasten with interest on a
particular distant spot. By following his gaze and
concentrating closely, I finally made out a moving
black speck on the far-off horizon.

"Car comin'," said the snake chief.

The car slowly drew near the mesa, and when
it was about two miles distant it stopped and a
man got out of it, and seizing what I took to be a
tent pole from the side of the car, went back a
little way and began flailing vigorously at a particular spot in the sand at the side of the road. The
Indian beside me winced as he watched his action,
and said: "Too bad. Bohana (white man) all
time kill poor snake. Pretty soon no snake for
dance ceremony maybe, and Hopis get no rain.
Long time ago, before too many bohana, plenty
snake, three, four bushel for dance. Now can
hardly find hundred in four day. Snake for long
time ago is Hopi brother. After dance he tell
Katchinas (spirits) send to Hopis rain for corn,

because Hopis is very nice people to dance with snakes."

That evening I heard the Government well-driller gleefully telling a group at the trading store at the foot of the mesa that he had killed a three-foot rattler on his way in that afternoon, but I noticed that the Indians in the group, among whom was the snake chief, listened with a depressed air to the driller's account of his adventure, and seemed sad at its termination.

THE ARTISTS AND THE SNAKES

THE ARTISTS AND THE SNAKES

IN WINTER time the Hopi Indians have many beautiful and significant dances and ceremonies. To see these dances and ceremonies and to try to paint them, two artists motored to Hopi from the town of Santa Fe, many miles distant. One of these artists, Heinrich Bollensch, had his origin in Germany while the other, Carlos Verencia, was of Latin extraction. Now there are no hotels or boarding houses at Hopi and these painters found it rather cold trying to live and paint in a tent, so they finally prevailed on the snake chief to rent them a little summer house that he had built at the foot of the mesa, convenient to his corn fields, where he lived during the growing season so that he could watch his corn.

The artists were delighted with this arrangement and felt themselves particularly honored to be allowed to live in this house, for the snake chief is one of the big men at Hopi, and they quickly posted cards to their friends in Santa Fe telling them of their good luck to be living in the house of the snake chief.

They found the unused summer house cold, so the next day the artists bought a cord of wood from one of the Indians and in the evening they built

37

a hot fire and soon had the room as warm as if it were August.

Carlos was frying their evening rasher of bacon on the old stove and Heinrich busied himself unpacking his tubes of paint when suddenly he said, "Carlos, I hear a noice. It sounds like a pumple pee was in our house already. Ya, I hear two pumple pees. I tink tey can have yet a nest maypee." Then he gave a yell that could have been heard a mile, "Mein Gott! Sind schlange!" and jumped to the table and from there leaped and caught a rafter and swung out over the room, far above the floor.

Carlos looked around in consternation, but being ignorant of German, did not understand what his companion had said. He thought that he had become suddenly demented and shouted, "Now what in Hell's the matter with you?"

Heinrich however soon enlightened him. "Der is schnakes in der home, Carlos. Look once by der rat holes in der corner ver I tink it is yet pumple pees vot sings." Carlos took one look and giving, if anything, a louder yell than had Heinrich, hopped to the top of the red hot stove, but not being able to linger there, he too jumped and grabbed a rafter. There the two swung and shouted, while below them in the now thoroughly heated room, sand rattlers and side winders began crawling from rat holes and cracks and slithering across the floor, raising their heads and looking at the two distressed artists. They sounded their rattles, while Heinrich and Carlos tried to out-do one another in their cries for help.

Now the Indians had heard the first yells of the artists and came running down from the mesa to see what the trouble could be, but when they came to the window and saw the two men swinging from the rafters they felt a delicacy about entering. They did not see the snakes and thought that the bohana (white) artists were doing some sort of exercises or that they were perhaps holding some sort of ceremony with songs and prayers in honor of their Katchina or God, a part of which required them to dance in the air. For the whites were always doing things that were even more unaccountable than this.

Finally one Indian, who had been away to school and who understood English very well, heard among a great many names, both celestial and infernal, the one word, "snakes," reiterated over and over again by Carlos (Heinrich by this time having lapsed entirely into German). This Indian turned to the snake chief and said "chua" (snake). Then the snake chief's memory began to function. He remembered that in the previous autumn he had become alarmed at the scarcity of snakes on account of the way the whites persisted in killing them and knowing how difficult it was now to procure a sufficient number for the snake dance, he had, whenever he came upon one in the fields, popped it into a bag and, as he passed his summer house on the way to the mesa, had raised a board in the flooring and dropped the snake into the hole beneath it to hibernate through the winter and so be ready at hand for the next snake dance time.

Forgetting all this when he rented the house to the two artists, he had not reckoned perhaps on the snakes awakening, but the snakes, sleeping underneath the floor, feeling the heat going through their cold bodies, warming their sluggish blood, thought summer had arrived, and had crawled forth seeking their master and brother, the snake chief.

The snake chief now quickly opened the door of the little house and grabbing up a snake bag from the corner of the room began nonchalantly clapping the snakes into it. He was much relieved that no harm had come to them at the hands of the unaccountable artists.

Heinrich and Carlos, seeing that the coast was clear, without further ceremony dropped to the floor and hurriedly gathering together their belongings, thrust them into the car and by driving all night arrived in Santa Fe, five hundred miles away, late the next morning.

Now in this situation of the two artists the Indians saw nothing amusing. They only saw that their sacred snakes had been jeopardized and thought that these men were more in sympathy with the culture of the Hopis than were the general run of the white people they had known and had considerately suspended themselves from the rafters to avoid stepping on and injuring the sacred snakes. They still have kindly thoughts for these two artists and consider them the most understanding and sympathetic visitors that they have ever had at Hopi, and should they return they would be more than welcome to join the snake clan and would be invited to participate in their most sacred dance.

As for the artists, Heinrich and Carlos, neither were *they* amused. When they arrived in Santa Fe, they slept a straight twenty hours in their own safe beds and when they awakened they read the following in that day's edition of the *Santa Fe New Mexican,* "Henry Bollensch and Carlos Verencia, two of our distinguished artists, write from Hopi to friends in Santa Fe that they are guests of the snake chief, and that they are enjoying, on this account, greater privileges than are ordinarily accorded to visitors at Hopi."

SAN JUAN DE LOS CABALLEROS

GREEN CORN DANCE

This dance in which both men and women participate is a summer dance and is a prayer that there may be plenty of rain for the growing corn and that there may be a bountiful harvest. The women's headdresses are cloud symbols and the men wear prayer plumes in their hair. The men also wear rain sashes hanging from their waists and bits of skunk skin about their ankles. The skunk skins are to prevent evil or witchcraft from entering the ceremony. Both men and women carry green boughs in their hands and in addition the men carry ceremonial rain rattles.

WHEN the first Spanish colony settled in New Mexico in the year 1598, their governor chose as his first capital a place now called Chamita, about thirty-five miles north of Santa Fe, the present capital. The Spanish governor called his capital San Gabriel.

The site chosen for the colony lay in the beautiful valley of the Rio Grande River, just above the point where it is joined by the Chama River, so the colony had water on either side. Beyond the valley to the east towered a high range of the Rocky Mountains called by the Spaniards "Sierras Grandes," and on the west rose a somewhat lower range called "Jemez."

Chamita was chosen by the Spanish governor for his capital because of a large, well-built Indian town or pueblo there, whose inhabitants were most friendly. These Indians were so well disposed toward the newcomers that they gave up their well-built adobe houses to them and moved across the Rio Grande and built themselves new houses in a new town. These Indians also showed the Spaniards how to lead the water from the river in ditches to irrigate their cornfields. The Spaniards were so impressed with the gentleness, kindness, and generosity of these Indians that they called this Indian town by the name of "San Juan de los Caballeros," or "Saint John of the Gentlemen," which name it still bears.

The San Juan Indians being so well disposed, the padres who accompanied the colonists found little difficulty in converting them to Christianity, and taught them to pray to the images of Mary and Jesus for help in time of need, in place of appealing to the old tribal gods.

Soon there arose desperate need for the Indians to call on the new gods for help, for a terrible drought descended on that part of New Mexico. The growing corn of the Indians began to turn yellow and dry, and the water in the river became too low to be led by the irrigation ditches to the new fields which the Indians had made on the higher bank across the river when they gave up their old fields to the Spaniards. Formerly, had such a situation as this arisen, these Indians would have had a great rain-making ceremonial dance and called on their old gods to send them rain. Now, with implicit faith in the magic of the powerful gods of their new friends, the chiefs of the clans went to the padre at the mission church and asked him to lend them the blessed image of the child Jesus. The padre inquired of them why they wished the image, and the chief of the corn clan answered: "We wish to carry the child Jesus around the cornfields, so that he can see in what a bad condition they now are, and maybe he will have pity on us and send the rain."

The padre agreed that the Christ child might go, and the Indians carried it with ceremony over all their fields, chanting and pleading with the little image for rain. Then they returned it to the padre at the mission and went home to await results.

Now as sometimes happens in New Mexico in summer, a great cloudburst rose over the Jemez Mountains and swept up the Rio Grande valley. It deluged the Indian fields and beat the corn to the ground, and worse still, hail followed the rain and completed utterly the destruction of the crops.

When the Indians saw what had happened they were very much cast down, for corn was their main staple of diet. That evening the chiefs held a council and early the next morning they again presented themselves before the padre and this time asked that he lend them the image of Mother Mary. The padre was surprised and inquired the reason for this request. The chiefs hesitated, but on his refusing to lend them the image without explanation, one chief said: "Padre, we wish to carry the Mother Mary around the fields this morning, so that she can see for herself what a mess her naughty little boy has made of our cornfields."

The Indians of San Juan say to this day that if you will look at the image of Saint Mary in the old mission church there, you can still see on her cheeks traces of the tears she shed from pity when she saw their ruined cornfields.

Ever since that time the San Juan Indians have had respect for the Christian gods, but they appeal to their own old tribal nature gods when they want rain for their growing corn. Then they dress in the ceremonial costumes as in ancient times and paint themselves with ceremonial colors, and carrying sprigs of green spruce they form in long lines and shake gourd rattles filled with seeds, to simulate the rain falling on the green corn leaves. So they dance from sunrise to sunset, to bring down the rain, while near by a large drum made of a hollowed cottonwood log, covered with rawhide, is beaten to imitate the thunder, and a chorus sings the ancient incantations.

HOPI QUARREL

ONE finds incongruous names among the Hopi
Indians. These names, for the most part, reflect
the personal taste of whatever missionary or school
teacher had first access to the Indian families at the
time of the births of their children. Of course a
Hopi has also an Indian name, so that he has to
suffer the humiliation of his English name only
when addressed by a white.

Percival probably received his rather too elegant
name from a slightly weak-minded, over-romantic
missionary or school teacher. He should have had
a robust name, for he was the heartiest eater and
the heaviest man that I knew among all the Hopi
Indians at the pueblo of Walpi. He was a grand
exception to most of the Hopi men, for they nearly
all are slender and short, while their wives are broad
and have figures both ample and, according to
white standards of fashion, over-nourished; but
since that is the prevailing style at Hopi any individual variation from it is subject to ridicule.
Ethel, Percy's wife, was as slender as he was broad,
and being thus unfashionable according to Hopi
standards they felt themselves somewhat ostracized,
and had built a little house down below the mesa
where Walpi stands, and near the spring.

When Percy was at home he kept Ethel supple and agile by constant running back and forth from the pot of stew simmering over the fire, and by grinding more corn to make more tortillas, thus increasing the difference in their sizes and making them a little more of a joke to the Indians of Walpi. Percy was blamed jokingly by the other Hopis, especially the women, because he ate too much and did not allow Ethel enough time to rest and grow fat.

For my part I liked both Ethel and Percy. Percy was a jolly, good-natured bear of an Indian with a laugh that rumbled in a region under his floating ribs, while Ethel was active and gay, always giggling or smiling, although I never went to their house that she was not busy about food; and while Ethel was thus occupied, Percy and I had many long talks about the "long time ago" of the Hopis.

One day, when I stopped at this house where I had always found sunshine and holiday, the fire was out, the mealing stones were silent, and there was a chill in the air and a feeling of desolation. Ethel was sitting amidst the ashes on the hearth with her hands resting idly in her lap and her eyes staring listlessly at the floor.

I knew that the moods of these Indians change quickly, but never before had I seen any one of them look so forlorn and hopeless, and in so short a time as did Ethel this day.

"What in the world is the matter, Ethel?" I asked her.

She turned toward me a most woebegone face and answered: "Oh, Percy, that old wolf, have leave me, and he go up on the mesa to the old home of his old mamma, and he say he never coming down here to my house any more. I wish the old bear die and starve to death all the time, and not have enough to eat."

"Well, that is certainly too bad," I sympathized. "What was the trouble that Percy left you?"

"Well he say, the bone needle is not where I say it is. He say it is where he say it is, and I say it to him the needle is not where he say it is, it is where I say it is, and he say then it is a lie that I tell him, it is where he say it is all the time. So I tell it to him, 'You are a bigger liar, for it is where I say it is and not where you say it is.' Then he get madder and he look where he say it is and it is not where he say it is because it is where I say it is and he get very, very mad to me then because it is where I say it is and is not where he say it is. He say to me I am big fool and put needle where he don't say it is and I am not any good for wife to him, for when he wish to sew his tobacco sack the needle is not where he say it is and he say then he don't like me any more because I am bad and wish to quarrel with him all the time and he say he go on mesa to his mamma house and leave me to be by myself all the time. And he say maybe he get for him another wife, not so crazy like me, and I say to him, like old Hopi say, 'Fat man lean wife, fat wife lean man,' for I very mad too, and he very mad and say bad word to me and I throw to him his shoe and he go away from here. Then I cry long time and am not mad to Percy any more, but am sorrowful and wish he come back, but he not come back."

It was none of my quarrel, but I felt badly over it, for I knew that these two Hopis were really very fond of each other. I did not wish to meddle in something that was none of my affair, but I did venture to say that I thought maybe Percy would come back again. "No," lamented Ethel, "I think he is not coming back because the needle is not where he say it is."

A day or two later I passed that way and saw a great deal of smoke issuing from the chimney of Ethel's house and a little later met Ethel coming from the spring with a jar of water. She was once more smiling and radiant. I greeted her and jokingly said: "Well, Ethel, you look happy again. Why is that, have you got another husband so quickly?"

"No," Ethel giggled. "Percy, he come home again."

"How did that happen?" I asked. "I thought he said he was not coming back any more."

"Well, I think so too for one whole day, and then I think his mamma she is pretty old and do not cook pretty good any more and cannot grind corn in very small pieces like Percy likes it, so I grind much corn and make piki, pikami and many cakes the kind Percy likes and put some sugar in them, and I make big stew with mutton and put much mutton fat into it and also much dried peaches. Then I give a little boy one cake and tell him to go to home of mamma of Percy and say to him I say dinner is cook. It is about dark then and pretty soon Percy come into my house very quiet like a shadow and don't say anything, only smell. Then I say very kind to Percy, 'Percy, dinner is cook,' and he eat everything I cook like he is very glad to do so and it make me very happy once more."

"Didn't he say any more, 'The needle is not where you say it is?' " I asked.

"No," Ethel giggled. "He say, very kind, it is nice weather and he think it will not rain that night."

A HOPI AFFAIR

A HOPI AFFAIR

Most of the time since Ta Ah's return from the Indian boarding school he had been kept busy by his father in a distant camp on the Hopi desert, taking care of a flock of sheep. Although he had been herded closely with many other Indian children in the prison-like school in California for several years, yet he was not lonely in this isolated camp, for he dreamed much of a wonderful Hopi girl he had met on the train returning home from school, and who lived in the pueblo of Walpi, which was near his own ancestral pueblo of Sichumovi.

One day Ta Ah's father came to the sheep camp to tell him that his mother wished to see him, and that he could go home and leave the sheep for the father to look after.

When Ta Ah arrived his mother met him with a happy smile on her face and said: "Ta Ah, I have good news for you. You are now old enough to be married and happy, so while you were away I made a nice surprise for you. I have found a nice smart girl, and I have married her to you and she is now your wife since this morning, and is waiting for you to come to her house."

Ta Ah was completely upset at this piece of

news. He knew that it was the Hopi custom for a mother to choose a son's wife for him, but he had been away at school so long that he had all but forgotten it, and anyway he had never thought of this thing happening to himself. Heartsick and depressed, he could not say a word to his smiling mother, but hurriedly left the house and hastened back toward the sheep camp, resolving that he would have none of this unknown wife who was not of his choosing.

Ta Ah's father was amazed at his return and asked him what the trouble was. Ta Ah related what his mother had told him, but his father was not surprised.

"Your mother is wise. She has found a good wife for you. Why do you run away from her? You have come back from school and need to marry, and it is the Hopi custom for a mother to find a wife for her son, for she knows which are the strongest girls, and who can grind the corn the finest. You have been home only for a short time and do not know who the best ones are."

"But, Father," replied Ta Ah, "I do not wish to be married to a wife that I do not love. I read in the white man's books that people should love one another before they get married."

"That," said the father, "is some more of the white man's nonsense that you young ones are al-

ways bringing home from the Government boarding schools. It is better our way, for then a boy
is always sure of getting a good wife. We will
sleep now, and to-morrow we will see."

Ta Ah could not sleep. His mind was too taken
up with his dilemma, and thoughts of Dawa, the
girl with whom he had fallen in love on the train,
kept him awake.

Long before day, Ta Ah slipped silently away
from the camp and went to a friend of his who had
returned from school the year before. Into this
friend's ears he poured his troubles. His friend
listened with a silent, judicious air and then said,
"You do not have to take that wife that your
mother has married you to if you do not wish to.
The Indian Agent says that all of the Hopis should
come to the agency and get themselves married in
the white man's way, so if Dawa Mana will have
you, the agent will marry you and your father and
mother can do nothing. You write a letter to
Dawa and ask her if she will marry you, and I will
take it to her."

Ta Ah took a pencil and paper and labored for
an hour, to the following purpose:

"Dawa Mana, Dear Madam, I am writing this letter to
tell you that I love you and will you be mine? I think you
are nice and pretty and both of your eyes shine like those of
a desert mice dancing in the moonlit. Your hair is beautiful
too like wool on sheeps backs but black and not white like

61

sheeps and your cheeks make me to think of the desert when the sun sets down on it. I have think of you all the time when the coyotes are not after the sheeps, for then I have to drive them away so that they do not hurt the sheeps. Yours truly,

Ta Ah.

P. S. Will you marry with me also? If you wish to do so, meet me when the sun rises to-morrow at Ishba spring and we will go to the indian agent and get married like white people do. My mother get me married already to a girl I do not know who, but I wish to marry only with you. Please answer to me soon,

Ta Ah.

The letter was delivered and a little later the friend returned with the following encouraging answer:

Ta Ah, Dear Sir, I am in receipt of your recent communication in which you inquire if I will marry with you. In reply will state that your proposal meets with my approval.

Yours truly,

Dawa Mana.

P. S. I will meet you when you say at Ishba spring. Also I think white man's way is another good way to get married too. P. S. I think of eagle whenever I see you.

Ta Ah was overjoyed, and he and his friend began to discuss ways and means. Now Ta Ah's friend was not only a friend in need, but he was also a friend in deed. He had a Ford. True, the Ford had seen its best days, but properly manipulated it could still slither its way through the desert sands, and the next morning at daybreak the two boys started to get it going. They took turns at

cranking, and finally the Ford coughed some of
the desert sand out of its throat and got going on
two cylinders, and as it warmed up a bit it picked
up on another, which was its usual rhythm. This
was sufficient for the boys and they reached the
rendezvous just as the sun came over the rim of the
desert. Dawa Mana was waiting for them, and in
an hour or more she was the lawful wedded wife of
Ta Ah.

With a wedding certificate according to the
white man's code and the agent's blessing, Ta Ah
and Dawa returned to Sichumovi. Dawa was entirely happy. Ta Ah too, but a bit perturbed. He
was thinking of his probable reception at home
after his breaking one of the oldest of Hopi customs.

When they arrived at his mother's house he
tremblingly entered it with his new bride, but con-
trary to his expectations his mother beamed with
smiles as she looked at them.

"You like wife I get for you? She is nice one
and can work."

The boy was nonplused at this reception, and
then Dawa giggled. He turned to her and said:
"Are you the wife my mother marry me to yesterday?"

"Yes," she giggled. "I want you for husband
first time I see you, you nice eagle man, and I

grind fine cornmeal to show your mother how well I can work, and she like it and take it, and everything is all right, but you do not come to my house, but run away and write to me you wish to get married for love by agent, and I think all right, if you like that way best I do not care, for it is a good way, too."

NOTE: When a Hopi girl takes a fancy to a man and wishes him for a husband she grinds some cornmeal very fine and carries it to the home of her prospective mother-in-law. If the meal is accepted and carried into the house it is a sign that she is acceptable as a daughter-in-law and she becomes forthwith the bride of the man she fancies, unless there is an older unmarried son in the family. In that case she becomes the bride of the older one.

AGO PO

THE SKUNKS

So'hn (skunk) symbolizes the black rain cloud with its white tip. Above the skunks in this picture is symbolized rain, the rainbow, rain clouds, and the sun (Tohn). Fur of the skunk is tied about their ankles by the men in most of the Indian ceremonial dances to prevent any evil or witchcraft from entering the ceremony.

AGO PO

It was one of those warm, sunny winter days which follow one another in a long procession in New Mexico. In the pueblo of San Ildefonso everything was very quiet, for the day before there had been a fiesta, and to-day the Indians were somewhat let down and were taking things easy. A whirlwind came up the Rio Grande and danced through the plaza, swirling up the dust in a great cloud. The Indians, seeing it coming, all instinctively stepped into their houses and closed the doors tightly; for witches stir up the whirlwinds and then ride on them where they wish to go, and no Indian wants a witch to step into his house from a whirlwind as it passes by.

While things were at their dullest in the pueblo this sunny winter day, a hired automobile from Santa Fe drove into the plaza and a woman stepped briskly out of it. Determination and purpose could be seen in her movements as she crossed the plaza. She walked in a straight line and without hesitation to the nearest house and knocked. An Indian woman opened the door, and bidding the stranger enter, placed a chair and asked her to sit down. Then she giggled a bit and stood uneasily watching her visitor.

The visitor took off her heavily lensed glasses, wiped them and replaced them. It could be seen that she had something important and momentous on her mind and was considering deeply how to make her approach. Finally she decided to be business-like and to the point.

She said: "I am going to write something on aboriginal and primitive life in the Southwest, and people in Santa Fe told me that you Indians of San Ildefonso could speak English and would talk more to white people about your myths and superstitions than any of the other Indians. Now will you tell me what the meaning of that dance was yesterday, where all the men came out of that round kind of a house, with hardly any clothes on and all painted with red mud, and jumped up and down in a row, while another group beat on a hollow log and shouted?"

"I do not know. The mens do it," answered the uneasy hostess with a nervous giggle.

"Well, do the men know?" asked the business-like visitor.

"Maybe. I do not know. They do not say it to me," was the reply.

"Do you like to live this primitive sort of life here in the pueblo?" was the next question.

"What you mean?" asked the Indian woman with an uneasy titter.

"Do you Indians like to live in a pueblo?" was patiently explained.

"We like it when people do not bother us all the time," was the smiling reply.

The visitor now stood up. Already ten minutes of the hour that had been set aside for collecting material were gone in futility. Then she asked: "Are there any men I can talk to?"

"I do not know. Maybe in the plaza you find mens," answered the Indian with another embarrassed giggle.

The woman stepped out into the plaza and gave it a quick survey. Over on the opposite side of the plaza she spied a rather large, heavy Indian sitting against the sunny side of an adobe house, somnolently soaking in the heat of the warm sunshine. The woman lost no time in placing herself before him. The Indian looked her over with basilisk-like eyes taking her all in—sensible shoes, silk hose, short green suit, well-developed chin and nose, thick-lensed glasses, and green, helmet-like hat. He was Ago Po, the keenest, wiliest Indian in San Ildefonso. He was the koshare, the fun-maker of the pueblo. Studying the weaknesses and foibles of humankind, both Indian and white, and taking advantage of them, was his business in life. He was always ready to amuse himself or others at the expense of someone else. Ago Po knew the woman before him immediately, not as an individual, but as one of a type. Often in the past he had secured a great deal of amusement from such as she; and when he had seen her alight in the plaza he had marked her as his own, but he was content to wait for her to come to him, as he knew she would in the natural course of events.

Ago Po now felt a resurgence of good humor and joviality, although to look at his stolid and forbidding countenance, one would think that he was contemplating mayhem. But Ago Po knew the nature of his victim and how to impart the proper thrill.

He now looked at the woman with sharp and glinting eyes and said "Howdy," before she could formulate her first question.

"How do you do," she replied. "Perhaps you can help me out. I want to find out something, first hand, about primitive and aboriginal life. Perhaps you will tell me something about you Indians and your myths and superstitions."

"Yes," said our fat Indian friend in a deep and rumbling voice. "I often tell white people things about us Indians. These other foolish Indians here want to keep everything secret, but I always say there is nothing about us Indians to be ashamed of. But when I tell things to people they usually pay me for my time. Even the Indians here pay me five dollars when I drive the witches away from the pueblo, for I am the big medicine man here."

The woman was thrilled and delighted to know that now she was going to acquire knowledge of Indians and their pagan beliefs at the real source, and very shortly Ago Po was five dollars the richer.

"Now," said Ago Po, "I will take you into the medicine house, so that the other Indians here will not see us and get mad at me for the things I am going to tell you and show you."

Ago Po then took his initiate into an old unused house that had belonged to his mother. The large room they entered was littered with the wornout and useless things that accumulate in an Indian pueblo, besides things that had belonged to his mother. Ago Po closed the door, as he said, to keep out the bad people that might hear the secrets he was going to reveal.

The first thing the woman spied was an old stone hunting fetish that resembled a hippopotamus, that sat in a niche by the fireplace. "Oh, what is that stone pig for?" she exclaimed as she went toward the image.

"Don't touch him!" commanded Ago Po. "If you turn him on his back all the stars will fall out of the sky. He is the sacred mountain lion of San Ildefonso. He was very big one time, but when the mountains catch on fire he dry up like this. A long time ago we live in the cliffs on top of the mountain at Tsankowi, and when we come down here to live, this mountain lion put all the stars in a buckskin bag to bring them, so we will have stars here too, but when we get nearly here he dropped the bag and the stars fall out of the bag into the sky where they are now—all crooked and not in nice straight rows like they used to be when we live at Tsankowi. Only three little stars are left in the bag, and the mountain lion set them in one little row in the sky."

All during this recital the woman was busy with pencil and notebook, and she finished with them just as Ago Po picked up a large old piece of flint and a small steel. "This," he explained, "is the lightning stone. When I see clouds coming up in the summer time and we Indians need rain, it is my work as medicine man to make fire with this stone, and the fire starts the lightning, which makes a hole through the water cloud and strikes the big water snake which rides in the cloud and makes him give a roar, which is called thunder, and his breath, when he roars, makes a wind which blows the rain down on our cornfields.

"When I want a water cloud to come I paint the other Indians with the sacred paint in this pot here and send them out in the plaza to dance and sing, while one old man beats a drum to sound like thunder. Then the big water snake in the river hears the noise and thinks the Indians are devils who are making the dance, and he makes a water cloud to ride in and comes over the pueblo so he can see the dance, and then I use the lightning stone like I tell you a little while ago."

"How very extraordinary," the woman said to this, and made some more notes under the heading, "Beliefs of the Aborigines of the Pueblo of San Ildefonso."

The woman next spied a small wooden figure, carved and painted to resemble a Franciscan monk in his habit, and known among the Spanish-speaking people in New Mexico as a santo bulto, or saint.

"That," said Ago Po, "belonged to my great, great grandfather. He was a great medicine man too in San Ildefonso. He did not like the padre who was here then, because the padre did not like our Indian ceremonies and called them witchcraft. So my grandfather made this figure to look like the padre. Then he would say some Indian witch words and stick a thorn in the figure, and wherever the padre was he would feel the thorn stick him in the same place and jump and say 'Diabolo!' very loud. The padre knew he was being witched, but he could find out nothing himself, for whenever he looked, my grandfather hid the figure. One day the padre sent to Santa Fe for a witch detective, and the detective soon found out what was going on, so my grandfather was arrested and tried in Santa Fe and hanged by the Spanish Governor there."

Next, Ago Po called his initiate to the center of the room, where there was a round post that helped to support the roof.

"This post," he explained solemnly, "we believe is the center of the world, and it is called the 'sun post.' It used to stand in our old place at Tsankowi, but when we moved here we changed the center of the world to here. This stick that is stuck in this hole on the north side of the post is the sun," he said, pointing to an old wooden peg which had been stuck into the post to hang clothes on, "and this hole it is in is the north sun hole, and this hole on the other side of the post is the south sun hole. When it gets too cold in the winter time and the sun goes too far to the south, I put the sun stick in the south sun hole and the sun starts back north, and pretty soon it gets summer time again, and when it begins to get too hot in the summer I change the sun stick to the north sun hole again, and pretty soon it gets winter again. One time the medicine man forgot to change the stick, and it was winter time for two years and the snow got five feet deep and everybody nearly freeze to death, and one other time he forgot to

74

change the sun stick and the sun got so close and hot that it set one of the Jemez mountains on fire and everybody have to take off their clothes, they get so hot, so I am very careful and do not forget."

Ago Po now became silent. He was thinking of the large pot of stew that his wife must have nearly cooked. Also he had had sufficient amusement and thought that he had given the woman her money's worth.

The woman glanced at her wrist watch and saw that the hour was up which she had dedicated to original research among the pueblo Indians of the Southwest. As she went toward the door she said, "Have you a wife?"

Ago Po, used to all sorts of questions, was a little bit amazed at this inquiry, but he concealed this feeling, and, ready to play the game to the end, replied, "I think she is down there yet," and stamped heavily with one foot on the hard adobe floor, which gave back a hollow sound.

"You mean that you killed your wife and buried her there?" the woman exclaimed in horror.

"Well, I don't know if I kill her or not, but I hit her on the head pretty hard and put her down there. But don't you tell anybody, for no one knows about it yet." And Ago Po looked at the woman with such a baleful gleam in his eyes that she darted through the door to the waiting taxi, where she collapsed on the back seat of the car as it moved away toward Santa Fe.

Ago Po then closed the door and went to his own house. As he ate the succulent stew his wife had cooked he chuckled happily. Finally his good-natured wife said to him: "You big bear, why do you laugh deep down in your belly like that all the time? Did you catch a chipmunk this morning?"

"No," replied Ago Po, "just a little white mouse, but it was a funny one and I played with it nearly an hour before I let it go." Then Ago Po chuckled again, and his good-natured wife giggled an echo.

As for the woman, she hastened back to Santa Fe and wrote copiously all evening on the subject of the myths and superstitions of the aborigines of the Rio Grande Valley, from material gathered at first hand by the author.

The next day she spoke of her trip to San Ildefonso and of the wonderful material she had obtained there to Mr. Chapman, the archaeologist at the museum in Santa Fe.

Mr. Chapman was politely puzzled at what she told him, until he found out the name of the informant. Then smiling, not too broadly or impolitely, he told her that Ago Po was the greatest joker and farceur among all the Indians he knew, and that, unless she had several years at her disposal for original research, she had better delve in the mine of the reports of the Bureau of Ethnology, as did most writers who wrote of Indians.

Now whether this woman has published anything of her "Life Among the Indians" or not I cannot say, but perhaps if you read enough books about Indians you may run across something written by her, for many people write things about the Southwest who see less than she did.

THE LITTLE FISH OF SAN JUAN

SPRING PLANTING DANCERS

These dancers perform a pantomimic ceremonial in which they symbolize the manner in which corn is planted, how it germinates and grows, and the way in which it is fertilized by the falling rain. The dancers are dressed and painted ceremonially. On their heads they wear turkey feathers and green leaves, about their necks and on their arms are green twigs, in their left hands they carry hollow gourd rattles containing pebbles which they shake to simulate falling rain and in their left hands they carry green branches, symbolic of growing things.

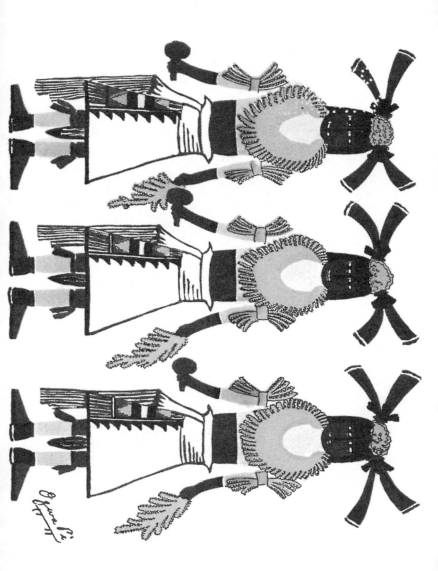

THE LITTLE FISH OF SAN JUAN

THE Indians of San Juan have not always lived on the Rio Grande River in New Mexico where they now do. Once, long ages ago, according to their history which is passed down from generation to generation by word of mouth, they lived far to the north in a place that they called "Cibobe," where it was very cold and where it seemed to grow colder and colder as the time went on. Finally half of the people, no longer able to endure the severe cold, gathered themselves together, and leaving their ancestral home of Cibobe and following the sun southward, went in search of a more pleasant place to live.

They followed the sun south for a long distance until they came to the great river, the Rio Grande. They then went along the west bank of this great river, through deep canyons and high mountain ranges, still farther to the south, until they came into a fine, wide, warm, and sunny valley where the ground was flat and great cottonwood trees grew on the bank of the river. Here they stopped and built themselves a pueblo of adobe on the west side of the river, where the soil was rich for the growing of corn and where there was plenty of water for irrigation.

They named their new pueblo Yuque Yunque, which meant "south warm place of the sun," and they called themselves the "summer people."

The other half of these people, who remained at Cibobe in the far north, became more and more miserable with the terrible cold as the years went by, and wished that they too had gone seeking a new home in the far southland with the rest of their people. Finally the increasing coldness, together with famine, forced them to leave their ancient home at Cibobe.

They attempted to follow the road taken by their brethren who had started for the south years before, but they soon lost the trail and wandered far off into the great plains to the east, where they found no warm valleys or beautiful river.

At last, after great hardships and after wandering wearily about over the wide plains, they turned westward and finally reached the east bank of the Rio Grande River and thence moving southward followed the river through the mountains until they came to the beautiful valley of Yuque Yunque.

Here they discovered the rest of their people across the river and were overjoyed, but they could only shout to them and reach out with their hands, for the river flowed deep between them. The newcomers stopped there on the east bank of the river opposite Yuque Yunque and built houses to live in, and the people of Yuque Yunque called them the "winter people," because they had stayed so long in the cold of the north.

Always from then on, the winter people and the summer people wished to be once more united, but the deep Rio Grande kept them apart. At last the medicine men of the two villages talked matters over between themselves as they stood on the two banks of the river opposite to one another and decided to build a magic bridge over the river, so that the winter people could cross over to the summer people.

The bridge was quickly built, for while the summer people had lived at Yuque Yunque their medicine men had been taught by Indians from countries far to the south the magic of the parrot, while the medicine men of the winter people had learned the magic of the magpie from Indians they had encountered in their wanderings to the east; so the medicine men of the winter people made a magpie feather so large that when they placed one end of it on the bank of the river the other end reached to the middle of the stream. Meanwhile the medicine men of the summer people of Yuque Yunque had made a parrot feather equally as large as the magpie feather, so that when one end of it was placed on the bank of the river on their side the other end reached out and united with the end of the magpie feather and thus formed a beautiful bridge over which the winter people could pass happily to Yuque Yunque. But what could be built by magic could be destroyed by magic. There was one very evil man at Yuque Yunque who was a wizard, and he did not want to see the people united and happy, and so, while some of the winter people were still crossing, he by his witchcraft caused the beautiful bridge to turn over and all of the people on it were thrown into the river, where he caused them to be changed into fish.

Now that happened a very long time ago; but never after that time would the people at Yuque Yunque eat fish, for fear of eating some of their own people, and the Navajo and the Apache knowing this story also would never eat fish, for the reason that they did not wish to be cannibals.

Many ages after the great catastrophe of the bridge, some of the Spanish people came north from Old Mexico into New Mexico to live and selected the valley of the Rio Grande at Yuque Yunque as the most beautiful place in which to locate.

The Indians of Yuque Yunque were so impressed by the Spaniards that they generously gave up their pueblo to them, and crossing the river on a new bridge that the Spaniards built, they made for themselves a new pueblo on the side where the winter people had formerly lived before they had all become united by means of the magic bridge. The Spaniards were so pleased with the Indians on account of this unsurpassed act of hospitality that they conferred on them the name of "the Gentlemen of San Juan," and by the name of San Juan these Indians have ever since been known.

Now, although what I have just told is a story in itself, yet at the same time it is a prologue to another story which would not be readily understood without it. We will call this sequel

The Mexican Cook and the San Juan Indians

A few years ago there was to be a great new highway built from Santa Fe, the capital of New Mexico, to the northern part of the state. Previous to this, the road had been only a track wandering in and out among the hills and canyons, dipping into arroyos and holes and trailing over rocks and sandy places.

First the highway engineers sent out gangs of men under foremen to build bridges and culverts and to remove rock, preliminary to the grading of the highway. When the road builders got to working up in the canyon of the Rio Grande, halfway between the pueblo of San Juan and Taos, they found that they needed more men than they had, so an engineer went to the pueblo of San Juan and recruited twenty Indians to help with the work.

A camp was established for these Indians, and a Mexican from Taos was installed as cook for the outfit. As a camp cook for Indians doing hard work, this Mexican was a success; for he could cook the sort of food the Indians liked in the way they liked it cooked. The Indians were quiet and industrious workers, so the foreman and his assistant were well pleased with their outfit.

One day after about two weeks of this highly satisfactory arrangement, the commissary truck that brought supplies from Santa Fe to the camp broke down on the road and left the camp without meat for the day.

At first José, the cook, was in despair at this disarrangement of his menu; but finally what brains he possessed came to his rescue and he opened an emergency ration box and took from it a dozen cans of tinned sardines. He then cut the tops from the tins and removed the sardines carefully, one by one, and placed them on a large plate, so that in spite of their long confinement in such very cramped quarters they still looked very much like fish when once they were released from their extreme proximity to one another, and José was much pleased and smugly satisfied with himself. He felt he should be congratulated for the efficiency and resourcefulness that he had displayed in this emergency.

When supper time came, the Indians filed in, tired and hungry from their day's work; but they took only one look at the heaped plate of slightly jaded sardines and bolted from the table, upsetting the benches in their haste.

Poor José was extremely bewildered at the behavior of his boarders, for Mexicans have never been able to grasp the idiosyncrasies of Indians. In this case he saw nothing to cause such abrupt and hasty action. Personally he much preferred sardines, as a delicious change from the regular routine of meat stew, and never once thought of attributing the flight of the Indians to the little fish.

The Indians went to the foreman and asked for and received their checks for pay to date. Then they took some amole, or soap root, and went up the river where there was a nice rocky pool, and there they took down their long black hair and began to give it a careful washing with the amole, as they always do on special occasions, and as they washed their hair, they chanted one of the weirdest of their primitive old songs.

Now it gives a Mexican of the outlying sections the creeps to hear an Indian chant in lonely places, and this fear, through many generations, has almost crept into their blood as a racial inheritance; and when José saw the Indians washing their hair with amole and heard them chanting, he became very nervous, for he knew that this was a sign from time immemorial among Indians that something outside the regular routine of things was about to occur. The foreman and his assistant heightened José's uneasiness by their serious and doleful expressions.

When the Indians had finished with their purification ablutions they started, still weirdly chanting, toward the camp, whereupon the foreman and his assistant walked over to José and solemnly shook hands with him. Then the foreman said very soberly: "Goodbye, José. You've been a good cook, and we hate to see you die this way before your time. Where shall we send your remains?"

José looked wild-eyed at the foreman. "Watsa matta wit damn Indians enaway they is mads at me?"

"Well," replied the foreman, "they told me you are a witch and tried to make them eat fish, and they said dead fish are same as dead brothers to them, and you hear them singing the war song, don't you?"

José gave one more wild look at the advancing Indians and then took a long dive into the bushes and rocks at the back of the camp and disappeared from sight. As for the Indians, they passed peacefully on their way to San Juan, twenty miles away, without even turning their heads in the direction of the camp; but long before even these good travelers arrived at the pueblo, twenty miles to the south, where the next day they were to take part in ceremonial dances, José felt himself safe among his own people in San Fernando de Taos, twenty miles away to the north.

THE HOLY WATER

THE DOG DANCE

This is a Tewa Pueblo Indian dance that is given just before a large public rabbit hunt. The ceremonially dressed and painted figure of the man represents tse'schal (dog). He is held on a leash and guided by the girl who holds magic prayer plumes in her hands which give her power over game. These Indians consider the dog very knowing about the ways of rabbits.

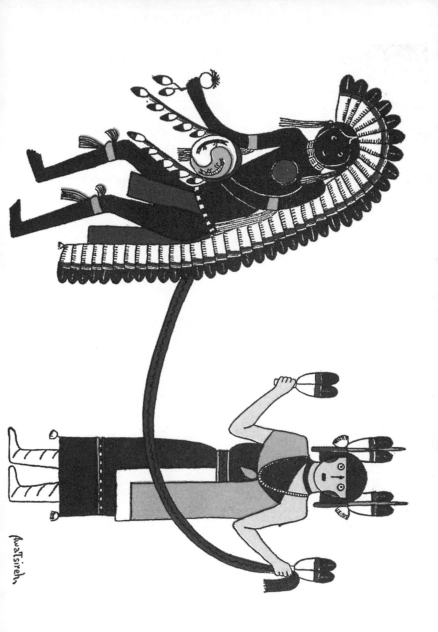

WHEN the Spanish colonists first came north into New Mexico their soldiers were dressed in armor and rode horses, and the pueblo Indians were much awed by them. Here were men, they thought, who must be great favorites of the sun, because they were so white. Also the incantations of their cacique or high priest must be very powerful, for they wore clothes which the hardest arrow or stone lance could not pierce, and they rode upon huge jumping beasts with large, fierce-looking mouths, set with very strong white teeth.

The Spaniards told the pueblo Indians that they had powerful priests who could intercede with the Great One Above, and who could, by holding a ceremony and sprinkling a person with a wonderful sort of sacred water, cause him, when he died, to go to a wonderful country up in the sky where he would live forever.

Upon hearing this bit of news the Indians of Nambé pueblo became very desirous to have one of these wonderful priests come to their pueblo to perform this miraculous ceremony for them and to introduce the worship of the white God at their pueblo, for the Indians were always glad to add the ceremonies of another god, if his power were great, to those they already had. So one of the Franciscan missionaries who had come north with the Spaniards to convert Indians to Christianity was assigned to Nambé pueblo.

The padre told the Indians that the great white God must have a church or kiva and that it must be grander than the ceremonial kiva of the Indian gods, so the Indians set to work with a good will, and soon a very large church was built, wherein the padre set up an altar and said mass for the benefit of the Indians, and baptized many of them.

Táhwi, the aged cacique of Nambé, who was high priest of the old Indian nature gods, was extremely interested in the white priest and his ceremonies. He went to the church many times and very closely studied all his actions and everything he said, not overlooking the slightest detail, hoping thereby to acquire the secret of these ceremonials and so be able eventually to perform them effectually himself.

Finally he came to the conclusion that the padre's ceremonies were not so very different from his own. The padre had a kiva or ceremonial room and in it an altar before which he performed certain obscure and mysterious ceremonies with strange looking objects, but instead of sprinkling sacred corn meal as a blessing, as an Indian priest would, he sprinkled a sacred kind of water. Now this sacred water was the mysterious thing to the ancient Táhwi. In it must reside great powers, he thought. Everything else he understood well enough, so at the first opportunity that presented itself, Táhwi purloined some of the holy water and took it to his home. There in a back room of his house he proceeded to experiment with it.

First he placed his finger in it to test it, but since nothing happened except that his finger was wet when he took it out, he tried rubbing some of it on himself to see the effect of that, but he felt no different, beyond a slight feeling of dampness, than he had felt before trying the experiment. Then he tasted the holy water, but it only seemed to him like the river water. He was a little puzzled at the lack of results from his experiments, but was not yet discouraged. He next called to his wife, who was grinding corn in another room, and ordered her to come in where he was. Then imitating the padre's tone of voice and words as best he could, he sprinkled his wife liberally with the holy water. This time, he got a quick and strong reaction coupled with a very good scolding. His wife told him that he had better not fool with the white priest's sacred water when he did not know its powers, or he might use it wrongly and bewitch someone.

This possibility rather frightened Táhwi, and he

took his wife down to the river and bathed her very carefully with sacred amole root, in order to wash off any curse that he might have put on her by the wrong use of the holy water. Then he sprinkled her well with sacred corn meal of his own blessing and told her that she was now all right again; but after that he left holy water alone and let the padre attend to ceremonies in the church, while he himself attended to performing Indian ceremonies to cure the sick, keep witches from the pueblo, lay ghosts, bring rain, make the corn grow, make game easy to catch, and a thousand and one other things that a successful cacique must do if his people are to prosper and be happy.

As for the padre, he was a real follower of the gentle Saint Francis of Assisi, kindly, tolerant and gentle with the Indians, so that he quite won their hearts. He baptized them, held mass for them, and when they died he sent them to the beautiful country in the sky where they could always be happy. As for the way they grew their corn, brought rain or found the game in the mountains and such little matters, he left that to them and he took no notice of their harmless little ceremonies. For he felt that they were a primitive people and that they could not suddenly give up all their old ways. He trusted to kindness, tolerance and time to win them entirely to his God.

Thus affairs went along happily for many years at Nambé.

The Wizard of Nambé

Finally there came a change at Nambé, and trouble came along with this change. The gentle padre was recalled and sent back to Spain, and a new sort of priest came to Nambé, very different from the former, always smiling padre. This new priest never smiled and he seemed never to be pleased with anything the Indians did. He scolded them and went about interfering with their most intimate affairs. He even attempted to stop all their ceremonies to their old nature gods, but was unsuccessful at this, and it angered him very much and he became very unpleasant to the Indians. The Indians became sullen and would not go to church. To them it was all very well to go to a pleasant country when they died, but here on earth they needed corn and rain and game, and many other things besides, and their old gods had always supplied those things when they were asked properly, but they doubted the white God's powers when it came to such matters. They explained very patiently to the priest, but only made him the more furious, and he told the Indians that their ceremonies were witchcraft and that their cacique was a wizard.

Then he had soldiers come out from Santa Fe and sent them into the kiva of the Indians, and had all the sacred ceremonial objects brought out and burnt in the plaza.

Táhwi, the old cacique, was arrested, taken to Santa Fe, put in prison and tried for witchcraft, for witchcraft was considered a great crime in those days. The priest came in from Nambé to testify against Táhwi. He said that Táhwi had bewitched him in such a way that he could not sleep at night, and that often he felt sharp pains in his back, especially when he was saying mass. Also that Táhwi had bewitched the other Indians so that they would not come to the church for mass.

Táhwi denied that he had bewitched anyone, so they put him to the torture. Now in New Mexico they had none of the machines for producing exquisite torture which the church in Spain used at that time, but they were not without resource. They tied the cacique's hands behind him and hanged him up by the thumbs. The pain was too excruciating for even an Indian to endure, and Táhwi confessed to taking holy water from the church and trying to use it. This was sufficient, and the old cacique was convicted and condemned to be hanged, along with another cacique from the pueblo of San Ildefonso, who had been condemned on a similar charge. It was in this way that some priests of that far off time attempted to stop the worship of their pagan gods by the Indians.

The Two Devils of Taos

The office of cacique at Nambé now devolved on Ahóa, who had been an acolyte of old Táhwi. Knowing the Spaniards and the enmity of the priest by this time, Ahóa took no unnecessary risks with his neck. When it was necessary to give an open ceremony to the old gods, Ahóa took the performers secretly, before day, to the old ruined pueblo of his people far up in the canyon, where there would be no spying priest to report them. But faster than the prayers for help that Ahóa sent to the old gods, troubles came to Nambé. The Spaniards in Santa Fe now arrived each year at harvest time and took more and more corn from the pueblo, and each year they forced more and more Indians to labor for them, making adobes and building houses for the people of Santa Fe; so that the people of Nambé grew to hate the Spaniards with a most bitter hatred, and since things did not prosper with the Indians, and many of them died of a disease they caught from the Spaniards, the Indians finally concluded that the Spanish priest was a wizard and that he had bewitched them.

Many years now passed, with the Indians of

Nambé becoming more and more depressed and having a harder and harder time. One evening Ahóa, now an old man, was sitting in his house meditating on the troubles of his people, when a strange Indian stood before him. The stranger had a large nose and a mouth that looked as though it had never smiled, and when he looked at Ahóa the cacique felt as though he could keep no thought hidden from this man. The stranger spoke and said: "I come from Taos pueblo with a message. Have the men who hate the Spaniards and hate the priest assemble immediately in the kiva, and allow no one to be there who cannot be trusted." Soon fifty Indians were seated around the walls inside the old round kiva that still stands in Nambé. All was in darkness, except for what little light came in through the square opening in the center of the roof, where the ladder entered.

The stranger stood just at the foot of the ladder, looking upon those seated about the room. As he looked at them, his eyes seemed to give off sparks of fire. At last he spoke, in a low, vibrant tone of voice.

"My friends, I am Popeé."

As he pronounced this name, his listeners all gave a slight start of surprise. They had all heard of this powerful and renowned man of San Juan pueblo, who had implacable hatred for the

Spaniards, and who had once been in prison at Santa Fe but had escaped and had gone to the pueblo of Taos to hide from the Spaniards.

"I have a message for you," he announced, if you have a great hate for the Spaniards."

He hesitated, and Ahóa said with much vehemence, "Even the air that the hated Spaniards breathe poisons us."

"It is well," resumed Popeé. "As you all know, since the priests of the Spaniards have come among us and built their kivas in our pueblos and made ceremonies to the white God, our own gods have gone scowling to their caves in the mountains, and have turned their backs on us and no longer hearken to our prayers, so that troubles are now with us always. My friends, which one among us wishes to go when he dies to that country in the sky of which the Spanish priest talks so much, and live with the Spaniards and be their slave?"

A low, sibilant hiss escaped from his listeners, and he went on.

"The Spaniards have taken land from us, they have taken our corn, they make slaves of us, they take our girls to cook for them and wait on them, they hang our priests and sell those who do not please them to work in the mines in the south. Their white God is good only to the Spaniards.

"My friends, in ten suns from now all the Indians in all the pueblos will kill all the priests and all the Spaniards in the pueblos and in the country around about. This will be very early in the morning, when the sun rises. Then we will all go to Santa Fe and kill all the Spaniards there, and then once more we will live in peace with our gods, who will come back smiling from their caves to help us."

Popeé ceased speaking and there was an intense stillness for a moment, and then Ahóa said: "My friend, it is hopeless. Before have the Indians tried this, but always has the white God of the Spaniards been too strong for us."

"It is true," replied Popeé, "that the Spanish God has always before been too strong for us, but this time it will be different. I have been making powerful ceremonies, and I have been able to raise up two great devil spirits to help us. On the appointed morning these two devil spirits will kill the white God, Jesus his son and Mary the mother of Jesus, who will then be unable to help the Spaniards, and we will then kill them all. I am now going to show you these spirits, so that you will know that what I am telling you is the truth."

Taking a small bag of sacred corn meal from beneath his blanket, Popeé made a large circle of corn meal about the foot of the ladder; then he took a quantity of some strange-looking material from a little bag he carried, and placing it on the ground in the center of the magic circle, set fire to it. A dense, pungent, thick smoke curled upward and out of the opening in the roof. Then Popeé chanted in a loud voice: "Spirits, come now and show these men of Nambé that you are real, and that on the appointed day you will kill the Spanish white God and his son Jesus and the mother of Jesus, so that they cannot help the Spaniards, and then that you will also help us to kill all the Spaniards."

Then Popeé threw something on the fire which gave out a very vile odor, and the smoke thinned and there at the foot of the ladder stood two tall, strange and grotesque-looking figures, their heads crowned with owl feathers, the insignia among the Indians of evil and witchcraft. At this awesome sight, the Indians present felt as though something were crawling under their scalps, and they were frightened nearly to death.

Popeé then addressed the figures: "Spirits, will you help us?" And one of the figures replied in a sepulchral tone of voice: "We will." Popeé then threw some more of the first material on the fire, and once more the dense cloud of smoke arose, and when it had cleared away the two figures were gone.

Popeé had no trouble in enlisting the Nambé

Indians to join his proposed rebellion against the Spaniards after they had witnessed this miracle, which the Spaniards later claimed Popeé had performed with the aid of two assistants whom he had left hidden outside the pueblo until they should get his signal.

On the appointed day the Indians of Nambé arose, and slaying the priest, hastened to Santa Fe, where, together with the other Indians, they attacked the Spaniards, and after killing many of them, drove the rest back across the Rio Grande River into old Mexico, whence they came. Then after a great celebration held in Santa Fe with the other Indians to rejoice over the defeat of the Spaniards, they returned to Nambé. There, after destroying the church and altar, they all went to the little river, where with amole root they scrubbed themselves vigorously to wash off the effects of the Christian baptism. They wanted to take no risk of going up to that country in the sky where they might have to raise corn for the Spaniards throughout eternity; for now they all thought that the wish on the part of the Spaniards to baptize them was only a scheme to be assured of plenty of Indian slaves in that country beyond death.

This happened in the year 1680. Years afterward the Spanish returned to New Mexico; but having learned a lesson, they treated the Indians in a much better manner, so that the Indians have lived peacefully with them ever since, and now even tolerate the worship of the white God, so long as it does not interfere with the worship of their own tribal nature gods.

TURTLE SHELLS

THE Indians of Hano, one of the Hopi pueblos, are somewhat different from the other Hopis and have a religion that varies considerably from that of those about them. They are comparatively late-comers to Hopi and had their origin on the banks of the Rio Grande River in New Mexico. They left their old home shortly after 1698 to escape from the Spaniards who were at that time settling in colonies in the Rio Grande valley and making vassals of the Indians there. The Hopis welcomed these Rio Grande Indians among them because they were good warriors and were on that account good protectors against the ever-marauding Navajos. From the Rio Grande the Hano women brought their art of making pottery and they are now the expert potters of Hopi.

One summer afternoon a group of Hano women were busy making pottery in the shade of some peach trees near the spring and as women the world over will do whenever they get together they were gossiping, and as gossips the Hopi women can not be surpassed. This is not to be wondered at for they live in such close contact with one another that each one can not help knowing what the other does.

Finally one of the Hano women turned to a woman of Walpi who was learning to make pottery by working with them and said, "Tabo Mana, you tell us something funny that happened at Walpi."

"All right," responded Tabo Mana, "I will tell you something that I think is funny, but you must not tell the Hopi mens I tell this story to you or they get mad at me and scold me. I will tell you about the bohana (white) lady of Baltimore and the turtle shells."

As Tabo Mana told the following story the women giggled and laughed, for to Hopi women, men are rather like grown-up children and are not to be held strictly accountable to the rules of common sense in the things that they do.

Last year there came to Walpi a nice bohana lady from a place she call Baltimore. She say she love all Indians so very much. She talk most all the time to the mens so we womens do not see them much at all. She ask mens all about Indian dances and katchinas and everything and she say all the time, "how lovely," when they tell her anything about Indians and their ceremonies.

She comes into our houses when we eat and she look over her glasses at us when we are sitting on the floor to eat and she say, "You eat your dinner? How nice." But she never eat with us. She say all the time she not hungry any and please excuse to her.

One day lady ask my husband will he sing nice Indian song to her and he say, "Yes," and he play on big drum and sing good, for he is got very strong voice. When he is finish she say, "How 'strordnry. I think it is marv'lous. What kind of song it is? Is it big war dance song?"

And my husban' say, "No. It is song about little blue butterfly that play in the wind with yellow flowers all day when the sun is shine in spring time and butterfly is happy all the time like little girl before she get married." And lady is then look some surprise and say, "How sweet."

She stay about a week maybe and when she is going away she say to old mens who are chiefs, "What do you need here most at Hopi to make everybody happy?"

Then the old mens talk together a long time and hold council and come back to lady and say to her, "We need turtle shells here at Hopi most of anything."

The bohana lady look very much astonish at this, but she say, "Very well, all right, I will send to you some turtle shells when I get home to Baltimore." Then nice bohana lady go away from Hopi to go home again and she say she going to write nice book about her dear friends, the Hopis.

Old mens all glad then because bohana lady going to send turtle shells to them. The reason why old mens are glad is because they got no more turtle shells to make more rain-dance rattles.

Long time ago Hopis live by big river at the south before they come to here. Down there where we live then are many little turtles in the river and the mens take the turtle shells about three or four inches long and dry them and then they tie the toes of deers on them to make some rattles and tie them on their knees so they rattle when they dance for rain, for turtles live in the water all the time and are good water medicine and when mens dance with turtle rattles tied to their knees the rain gods hear the noise and know the Hopis need rain for corn and send it to them pretty quick. But that so long ago nearly all the turtle-shell rattles the Hopis bring to here are break or wore out, so all the mens are glad Baltimore lady is going to send for them some more soon.

One day old chief of corn clan is get letter from Baltimore lady and it say, "Turtle shells are sent." Then all the mens go to the kiva and get ready for big rain dance and when box come they open it very quick to see turtle shells and all the mens are very surprise when they see. It is very big box and in it are two turtle shells more than two feet big. Mens all say, "Ah!" and look once more astonish. Then old mens say, "What to do? Shells too big to tie on knees for dance," and other mens say, "Yes, are too big for dance with."

At first they not know what to do, but pretty soon they take the shells to ceremonial kiva to talk some more and old corn clan chief say, "These turtles are father and mother of all the turtles and maybe they are very big medicine for rain." Then he put some prayer feathers on big turtle shells and pray to gods for rain and next week so much rain is come it wash our houses nearly down.

Then old men say it is too much medicine in big turtle shells and they take big turtle shells out from the kiva and bury them in the cornfields so rain is come there and not on the houses to wash them down.

Now mens do not ask kind bohana ladies for turtle shells any more. They say maybe it is better they go down themselves to big river in south and get some more little turtle shells for rattles. Then they can make just as much rain as they need and not try to make rain with bohana turtle medicine they do not understand and make too much rain maybe.

The Hopi woman told this story in English so that the bohana (white) visitor could understand it.

COCHITI ANCIENT HUNTING DANCE

Cochiti Ancient

Hunting Dance

COCHITI ANCIENT HUNTING DANCE

COCHITI is a pueblo of the Keres Indians and is situated on the west bank of the Rio Grande River about thirty miles below Santa Fe. At the back of the pueblo, to the west, rises the high range of the Jemez Mountains, while before the pueblo flows the broad and muddy Rio Grande. For long ages these Indians have farmed irrigated fields along the river and have depended on the produce of these fields for the most of their food.

At the pueblo of Cochiti are performed some of the most beautiful and interesting interpretations of their ancient legends and myths. In January 1929 they performed one of these dramas which they call, "Ancient Hunting Dance." This is an interpretive dance that is seldom given, and it is performed by several of the different clans of the pueblo, taking place in the old plaza surrounded by the houses of the Indians.

During this dance Lorenzo, one of the Cochiti Indians, sat by his white visitor and explained its significance as follows:

This is a very old ceremonial dance telling about something that happened a very long time ago. My father used to tell me that long time ago the

Indians brought trees from the mountains when they gave this dance and set them up in the plaza like a woods and that one of the trees always had squirrels and birds in it, and the Indians, who were dressed as eagles, deer, hunters, and grandfather spirits, danced among the trees, but there are not so many of us now and we do not bring trees from the mountains any more. The meaning of this dance is that a long time ago, before any white people came to this country, there was a big hungry time and we have nothing to eat, because the grasshoppers came here and eat up everything that is green, so that we have no corn. When our hunters went out to hunt for deer for the starving people they could not find any, for the deer had run away to the Jemez Mountains and could not be found.

Then a cacique beat on the big Cochiti drum and called to the Great Spirit to look down upon his people and have pity on them because a wizard had made grasshoppers to eat all the corn and had hidden the deer where they could not be found by the hunters.

The Great Spirit looked down on the starving Indians and felt sorry for them and sent four sacred eagles, two man eagles and two woman eagles, to find the deer for the hunters. The eagles then fly over the mountains till they find the deer where they are hidden in a deep canyon and they hover in the air above the game. Then our hunters go to where the eagles are and they see the deer in the canyon but they do not know what to do, for they can not get down into the canyon where the deer are because the walls are too high and steep.

When the Great Spirit see what is the trouble and that the hunters cannot go to the deer because the canyon is too deep he sent two of the spirits of our grandfathers who had been our caciques back from the great country in the west, where they had gone when they die, to help the hunters. When our grandfathers come back from the west they always do funny things, for they are always happy when they are dead and they wish to make us laugh and be happy also. When the two spirits come back to help the hunters they are dressed like funny hunters and have very crooked bows and arrows like you see the two koshares in the dance. The two spirits went up by the deep canyon where the deer are hidden and they act like hunters that do not know how to hunt well and they do very funny and foolish things.

They see a squirrel sitting in a tree and they act like they are trying to creep up on it and surprise it, but they fall down over stones and bushes and make very much noise. Then they both of them shoot at the squirrel but one arrow go crooked and hit the other grandfather and the other arrow shoot only three feet and fall on the ground and do not hit anything at all. When the squirrel see this he think it is very funny and he is laugh very loud. Then the grandfathers see a magpie in another tree and they shoot at him too, but one arrow is hit a rock on the ground and the other one go behind him who shoot and he stumble and fall down and the magpie laugh very loud at them also.

The deer down in the canyon hear the squirrel and the magpie laughing and they come up to the top of the canyon to see why they are laughing and they see the funny hunters and watch them a little while. The grandfathers are then shooting at a stone which they say they think is a rabbit, but all the time their arrows go very crooked and they do not hit anything. Then the deer say to one another, "Indian hunters are no good. They can not shoot anything. There is no use for us to be afraid of them any more." The deer all go away from the canyon then to get more grass. The sacred eagles of the Great Spirit see the deer going away and follow them to where they go, and our good hunters, the wise serpent people and the straight-shooting bow people, go where the eagles fly and pretty soon they see the deer in a valley and get them and bring them to the pueblo and then we have plenty to eat and do not starve any more.

Sometimes we have this dance to show the people the story and to let the Great Spirit know we are glad and remember what he do for us that time.

This hunting dance of Cochiti, the significance of which Lorenzo described quite adequately, was staged very beautifully. The first group of dancers to appear were two women and two men costumed to represent eagles. Eagle plumes and paint were used freely in their make-up. These dancers mimicked eagles in flight and in hovering over different spots. It could easily be seen that they had made intensive studies of the birds to be able to reproduce their movements with such nicety. The eagle is the most sacred bird of the pueblo Indian. It is the messenger of the Indian gods, and they use its plumes in all their ceremonies.

While the eagle people were moving about the plaza two Indians of the koshare society, who represent spirits of the Indian ancestors in the ceremonies, came out dressed as hunters, but in very ludicrous and tattered costumes and with clumsy and useless bows and crooked and blunt arrows, and pretended to be hunting. They clowned all the movements of hunters and were extremely clumsy at all they did. They stumbled over one another and even over their own feet. Their crooked arrows would shoot only a few feet and they never hit near anything aimed at.

Following the koshares two groups of Indian hunters entered the plaza. They were dressed in buckskins and had their bodies painted with ceremonial colors and designs. One group was made up of members of the plumed serpent clan and each individual of the group wore a kilt with plumed serpents painted on it and each had a fan-shaped bunch of eagle feathers fastened to the side of his head. The other group was made up of members of the bow clan and each member wore a strung bow, decorated ceremonially with eagle feathers, tied to the top of his head. All the members of both these groups carried very good hunting bows and arrows in their hands. These groups of hunters went gliding about the plaza, weaving in and out, imitative of Indian hunters, and when they reached the other side of the plaza two Indians, costumed to represent deer and wearing deer horns on their heads, appeared before them and altogether, eagles, deer, and hunters danced, while at one side a large group of Indians sang the ritual songs and a smaller group beat the large, old tribal drums in unison with the steps of the dancers.

THE HOPI FAMINE

THE HOPI FAMINE

At Walpi I often noticed a little, old, wrinkled Indian with an ingratiating grin on his face. With a quick nod to me he would scuttle into the low, hole-like doorway of one of the oldest houses of the pueblo, disappearing like a badger in his burrow. I noticed him in particular, for he seemed different from the other old Hopi men. He was less dignified, more self-deprecatory, and had an ingratiating air, as though trying to placate all with whom he came in contact. He was also much shorter than the other Hopi men, and had the appearance of having at some period been stunted in his growth, perhaps by undernourishment.

One day I absent-mindedly greeted this old Indian in Spanish, as I often did the older Indians among the Spanish-speaking people of the Rio Grande valley. Immediately his whole manner changed. He ran to me, and grabbing my hand poured out Spanish words so rapidly that I could scarcely catch their meaning. Finally he calmed a bit and began speaking more coherently, and as we sat on a large stone he told me his story, which I found the most amazing of any I had heard at Hopi. This story I have translated into English from his Spanish, and arranged it so that it may be followed more easily.

The Famine

A long time ago—just how long no one knows, for the Hopis kept no calendar in those days, there was a great drought, with terrible famine as the consequence, in the Hopi country. Those of the Hopis who still had a supply of corn from the previous harvest conserved it carefully, while those who had none scattered far and wide in search of any sort of food that would keep them from perishing.

In Walpi at that time there was a poor, widowed Indian woman with two small boys. She had raised but a scant supply of corn the previous year, so when the terrible famine came she was entirely without food for herself and her children. For a while the other Indians gave the poor woman corn, but soon they had to look to the future feeding of their own, so she was compelled to search elsewhere for food.

The poor woman was now desperate. She saw her two boys growing daily weaker, while she herself starved. At last, in her terrible dilemma, she decided to make a desperate attempt to reach the pueblo of Zuñi in far-away New Mexico, so that she could appeal to the Indians there for help.

The three of them started out on their long and

arduous journey. Little Mungwu, the older of
the two boys, walked by the side of his mother,
while she carried on her back his small brother,
who was too little and weak to walk. The mother
herself was so weak from lack of food that she had
to stop very often and place her burden on the
ground and rest. To add to her distress the child
cried almost constantly from hunger. Little
Mungwu was just old enough to partly realize the
situation, and bore himself as stoically as possible,
although hunger gnawed at him constantly, but
the mother in her anxiety scarcely noticed her own
discomfort.

As they painfully put distance between themselves and the Hopi villages they began to find a
few edible roots, and now and then some of the
edible fruit of the prickly cactus, but these things
were so affected by the drought that there was
little nourishment in them. Whenever his mother
stopped to rest Mungwu went about searching for
something to eat. Once he found a nest of desert
mice, and the starving little family were not too
nice to accept what little nourishment they offered.
At another time Mungwu snared a pack rat with a
string made of yucca fibre, and they made a supper
of it. In their desperate hunger they could dis-
dain nothing that might contain even the slightest
degree of nourishment. One day Mungwu dug at a

burrow into which he had seen a rabbit disappear until his fingers were raw and bleeding. At last he got it out, and it was none too plump, but the next day the little family was stronger, and able to go a mile or two farther than usual.

At last, after many weeks of unbelievable hardship, they arrived, almost dead with fatigue and hunger, at Zuñi. There the Indians received and cared for them, for Indians are always hospitable when they have food, and since the Zuñi Indians irrigate their fields with water from a river, and are not entirely dependent on seasonable rains for their cornfields, as are the Hopis, they had plenty to eat. The mother and her two boys were well cared for until they were somewhat recovered from their starvation and fatigue, but as hospitality among Indians covers only a restricted period of time the mother had to begin to work to support her small family, and throughout the winter she ground corn with the laborious mealing stones for the different Indian families, that she might earn a sufficient daily dole of meal for the support of her own.

At last spring came, and the Hopi woman longed to return to her own people and her old home at Walpi, and again plant her fields, but to do this she must have corn for seed and for food, and with all her work she had scarcely been able to earn enough to support herself, much less put anything by. At last, in her desperation, she traded little Mungwu to a Zuñi Indian, in exchange for all the corn that she could carry, and leading the smaller boy, who was now able to walk, she started on her long return trip to Hopi.

Little Mungwu was now kept busy by his new master, hoeing corn, carrying wood, and doing many other tasks that are necessary in an Indian household, so that memories of everything Hopi gradually became blurred in his mind.

After Mungwu had been at Zuñi for nearly two years a Mexican from Albuquerque came with a train of burros on a trading expedition. He had bright-colored calicoes, kerchiefs, and gaudy shirts. These things he traded to the Indians for tanned skins, furs, and silver. The Indian who owned Mungwu coveted a red shirt, but as he had nothing else that the Mexican would accept for the shirt he finally exchanged his little Hopi slave for the red shirt and a piece of calico.

Little Mungwu got on well with the Mexican, for he was quick and intelligent and he tried his very best to please his new master. His job was to look after the burros, to keep them moving and see that they did not stray from the road. The Mexican's name was Baca, which means cow in Spanish, and since he did not fancy Mungwu's Indian name he renamed him "Chico," which means "little one" in Spanish, and as "Chico Baca" Mungwu was known for many years.

Chico Baca worked for his Mexican master in Albuquerque until he was grown, and then, the Mexicans being no longer allowed to keep Indian slaves, Chico became a free man. By this time he lived very much as did the Mexicans. He spoke Spanish fluently, had been baptized into the Catholic church and was very much interested in the Mexican girls of Albuquerque. But they scorned his attentions, and only made fun of him because he was undersized and was a full-blood Indian. They called him Little Coyote and Monkey Face.

Chico took all his repulses good-naturedly but persisted in his admiration for the girls, and at last he was rewarded. Dolores Vigil, a Mexican señorita who was cross-eyed, marked by smallpox, and had a vile temper, being avoided by all the young Mexican bloods accepted Chico as her lover. She was five years his senior and they were married in the church.

Chico, however, was not happy with his new bride. She abused him dreadfully and applied to him such uncomplimentary names as coyote, rabbit, monkey, and burro. She kept poor Chico always on the jump because of her demands for money, and it was from this period that a placating grin became a fixture of his face.

Had it not been that at that time the Santa Fe Railroad Company was extending its lines by way of Albuquerque to the West coast, Chico Baca might have continued in the clutches of his Mexican virago for the rest of his days. But, hearing that silver might be earned by helping the iron horse on its way, Chico applied with an earnest air to the track-laying boss for a job. The foreman looked Chico over and told him he was too little for the job he asked for, but he made him a helper to the cook of the outfit, and from then on Chico was busy rustling wood and water and peeling potatoes.

Chico was quite happy in his new employment, and as long as the work was close to Albuquerque he went home every night and dutifully turned his wages over to his wife, but as the construction of the road moved farther toward Gallup he could get home seldom, and soon he neglected to go home at all.

Finally the rails were laid as far as Holbrook, which is about eighty miles directly south of the Hopi reservation, and some of the Indians came down to the camp there to try to get a job working on the construction of the railroad. By this time Chico's memory of his childhood had all but vanished from his mind, but when he heard the

Hopis talking he found that he understood much of what they said.

He then spoke a little to them in their language, and they were amazed at that and began to question him concerning his past. It chanced that one of the Indians was an uncle of Chico, and he quickly recognized, from the answers to the questions put to him, who this young man was. He then told his nephew that he was a Hopi and that his name was Mungwu. The sound of this name struck a responding chord somewhere in Chico, and memories of his childhood began to return to him.

Mungwu, as the Indians began to call him, was told by his uncle that many years before he had made a trip to Zuñi searching for his nephew, and had been told there that he was dead.

The uncle had no difficulty in persuading his newly found nephew to return with him to Walpi. When they went to the home of Mungwu's mother she at first paid no attention to this stranger Indian. She had long ago given up Mungwu for dead, and her other boy had died soon after she had returned from Zuñi many years before. When she did discover who this strange Indian was she was frantic with joy, and would not let him leave her side for many days. They recalled together the incidents of their terrible journey to Zuñi, and she told Mungwu the story of her long trip back to Hopi. She also told Mungwu that since that great famine, when so many of the Hopis had died, all the people there kept a two years' supply of corn stored up, for fear of another famine, and showed him her own supply, neatly piled up in the store room.

Mungwu remained at Walpi, but he never re-married. This was not because he was restrained by memories of his Mexican wife, but because the Hopi girls were not kind to him, partly on account of his appearance and partly on account of the elaborate and affected manners he had acquired by living so long among the Spanish-speaking Mexicans.

When among men Mungwu got a certain compensation for the rejections of his love making by the Hopi girls, by bragging of the great beauty and kindness of the wife he had left in Albuquerque, forgetting, for the time being, her crossed eyes, her disfigured face and her terrible temper, but he never for a single moment considered rejoining her, for even in his moments of greatest enthusiasm he never forgot the constant nagging demands she had made on him for money, a commodity fortunately that was not necessary for happiness at Hopi.

THE TURK OF PECOS

THE TURK OF PECOS

ONE spring morning in the year 1541 the Indians of Pecos, the largest pueblo in New Mexico at that time, witnessed what was to them an amazing and wonderful sight—the coming to their town of Coronado and his conquistadores. Under his command Coronado had the finest army ever assembled up to that time in America. It was composed of three hundred Spanish noblemen and gentlemen of fortune in complete armor, and with over a thousand Mexican footmen. Coronado, as leader, was encased in gilded armor of the richest sort, and no Indian arrow, lance, or war club was able to penetrate or even make a dent in his own or in the armor of his companions, so that each of them went safely about among the Indians inside his own private fortress.

These Spanish conquistadores had come north into New Mexico upon hearing rumors of wonderful cities there, full of gold and other treasure, which they hoped would prove even richer than anything yet found in Peru and Mexico, where the Spaniards had recently plundered enormous treasures of gold and silver.

So far, in New Mexico, they had been bitterly disappointed, finding only adobe Indian pueblos and no sort of metal whatever. But recently Coronado's spirits had been somewhat revived by stories the Indians told of wonderful cities far to the northeast of New Mexico, where gold was the most common of metals.

The best stories of the Grand Quivíra, the names of the wonderful cities, were told Coronado by a slave of the Pecos Indians who had been captured far off on the plains to the east by the Comanches and sold to the Pecos pueblo. This slave claimed to be a native of the cities of the Grand Quivíra and told Coronado stories thereof which would outdo the stories of Sindbad the Sailor.

Coronado, who thus far had been so bitterly disappointed, listened avidly to the stories of the Turk, as the Spaniards had dubbed the slave on account of his physiognomy. Some of the Pecos Indians had told him that the Turk was given to exaggeration, but he believed the stories because he wished them to be true. So here was Coronado come to Pecos to prepare for his long journey into unknown country in quest of the great Eldorado—the Grand Quivíra.

The Indians of Pecos welcomed Coronado in their best manner. They gave him provisions to take with him and furnished him with guides and interpreters, including a free gift of the Turk. The people of Pecos were glad to see Coronado started on his way, for it was a great undertaking for them to entertain and feed such a host.

The plan of the Indians was that the Turk was to lead the Spaniards out on the dry, waterless plains in what is now northern Texas, where they and their horses would all perish of hunger and thirst. The Turk, with this in mind, even tried to dissuade Coronado from loading the pack horses with many provisions, telling him that he would need the horses to bring back the gold from the Grand Quivira, and that to load them with provisions would needlessly tire and weaken them.

The Turk also had a grand scheme of his own. From the time that he had first seen Coronado he had been extremely envious of his gilded armor, and his plan was that when Coronado was good and dead on the plains he would move into his gilded armor. He thought how wonderful it would be to get inside this little "iron house" and be able to go where he pleased, and ever after be safe from arrows and all other Indian weapons.

As the army moved away from Pecos, the Turk rode beside Coronado and further regaled him with the wonders of the Grand Quivíra, to all of which Coronado listened eagerly; and when the Turk would tire, Coronado would encourage him to greater extravagances. Not that the Turk needed much encouragement, for his imagination had no bounds. He told Coronado that in Grand Quivíra gold was so common that only the lower classes ate off gold plates, while the rich and the king preferred wooden plates, because they considered them rarer and more beautiful. He said that gold was so common that anyone using it for ornaments was looked down upon. Wash-basins of gold were used, but people kept them behind the houses, where they could not be seen, and rather than bathe in them, the people would go and wash in the river. The only article of gold the king would allow in the palace was a cuspidor. Thus was Coronado's interest kept up day after day on the long journey, and as he rode along and drank in these stories with all his ears, the Turk eyed his gilded armor and wondered why anyone possessed of such a marvel should ever desire any other thing.

At night, when the army dismounted, the Mexican Indian servants hurried to the Spaniards and helped them out of their "iron houses." Otherwise, should they attempt to lie or sit on the ground anywhere in eastern New Mexico, one of the large, savage red ants of the desert was sure to find a crevice in a joint of the armor and make it more unpleasant for the occupant than would a hundred wild Indians with arrows and spears.

The wonderful hopes and plans of the Turk went awry. Instead of starving, the Spaniards found plenty of buffalo on the plains, for these animals had wandered farther south at that season than they usually did, and because that happened to be a rainy summer there was also sufficient water to keep them going. One day they met a tribe of plains Indians, who told Coronado that he was going too far southeast if he expected to go to Grand Quivíra, so Coronado turned toward the north.

The Turk was very plausible. He told Coronado that he had lost direction because always when Indians wish to go in a certain direction they keep shooting arrows straight ahead in that direction, and follow the arrows, lest they circle or bend in the march, and that in this case that had not been done.

Coronado accepted the explanation with reservations and kept on traveling north until he came to the Arkansas River, in what is now Kansas. This he crossed where Dodge City now is, and turned and followed the river east for a long distance. As he traveled, he inquired the way of all the Indians he met, until turning north again he finally approached the Grand Quivíra, a little west of where Kansas City now stands.

At last, after five months of arduous travel, Coronado arrived at the far-famed Grand Quivíra —Grand Quivíra, where all the houses were built of stone, and where gold was too common for the better class of people to use, and where the people, even the poorest, dressed in finely woven fabrics—finer than anything the Spaniards had.

What was this Grand Quivíra that Coronado found? He found a little muddy town on a little muddy river. The houses were built of thatch made from the blue-stem prairie grass of the Kansas plains. He found the village inhabited by a tribe of half-naked Indians, now known to have been the Wichitas. These Indians were scantily dressed in buffalo skins, and they raised a little corn, which they ate when it was too much trouble to find buffalo meat.

Coronado drew his army up before the village and looked at it with a soured expression on his face. He had wandered over fifteen hundred miles on horseback, living along the way on half-cooked buffalo meat and wearing his little "iron house" until he had deep calloused places wherever it touched his body. He had been ever hopeful throughout the journey, and here was this Grand Quivíra which was not half as fine as the poorest and most miserable pueblo in New Mexico.

But Coronado was a thorough man. From the largest grass house he had the king brought before him, and through another interpreter whom he had brought from Pecos, instead of through the Turk, he asked the king if he had any great treasure. The king answered that he had the greatest treasure of all the Indians in the whole country. At this news Coronado immediately cheered up. He dismounted, and with his lieutenant and the interpreter entered the long house of the king.

The king made them welcome to a seat on a buffalo robe and then said something to his servant, who brought a large old stone pipe and a large leather bag and gave them to the king. The king took some very black tobacco leaves from the bag, with which he packed the bowl of the pipe, telling Coronado in the meantime, through the interpreter, that this tobacco was very strong medicine for peace. He said that it was grown especially for him, up by the big muddy river in the north, and was the largest and blackest tobacco grown. When the bowl of the pipe was well packed, the servant brought a coal of fire and the king got the pipe well started, expelling great clouds of smoke with "ahs" of satisfaction. Then he handed the pipe to Coronado. Coronado took one puff and nearly strangled, and his head swam for several minutes afterward. The result on the lieutenant was the same, for the tobacco was quite different from the mild tobacco of old Mexico, but the king received the pipe back and smoked with great gusto. Coronado and the lieutenant politely refused the next round.

Coronado finally became impatient, and his curiosity getting the better of him, he asked to see the great treasure of the king.

The king reluctantly laid aside the pipe, and with a royal gesture gave a command to the servant, whereupon the servant went to the corner of the room and took down from the ceiling, where it was suspended by loops of thong, a section of cottonwood log, nicely hollowed out and well fitted with a wooden lid, wrapped tightly to the log by rawhide thongs. This he respectfully placed before the king.

The king carefully undid the thongs of the lid and lifted it off the box, with Coronado and his lieutenant craning forward to catch a glimpse of the contents. The king now reached in and began taking things from the box.

The first thing he held up was a lock of black hair attached to a small piece of dried skin. "This," he said, "I consider my one greatest treasure. I took it from the head of my greatest enemy, the chief of the Leyas beyond the great south river. This I also consider a great treasure," he continued, holding up the dried claw of a crow. "This the medicine man cut from a witch crow, and it is very good medicine against witchcraft."

Then he took from the box a small, rudely hammered piece of copper with a string run through it. This he said was a charm against lightning, and he generously gave it to Coronado, telling him that it might come in handy some time. The next thing was a little skin bag of corn pollen, which the king said was good medicine to make the corn grow.

Coronado listlessly watched the king take out little curiously shaped stones, pieces of bone and shell, strangely whittled sticks and little bags of colored earth, the uses of which the king explained at length. When he had finished Coronado arose, and thanking the king kindly for the exhibition, left the house.

Coronado had now only one great pleasure before him. Going to his tent, which in the meantime had been set up, he sent for the Turk. The Turk was found haranguing the populace of Quivíra, telling them to rise up and slay the Spaniards, and he would give them everything but the gilded armor of Coronado.

Two Spanish soldiers rudely pulled him away from his soap-box oration and took him to Coronado's tent, where Coronado had already given his instructions. When the Turk came into the tent the loop of a running knot of a rawhide lariat was dropped quickly around his neck and the ends drawn taut by two strong Mexican Indians. Soon the Turk was as Coronado wished him and had pictured him several times during the day. This vision was the only thing that had made the day bearable to him.

A hole was now quietly dug in the center of the tent and the Turk was laid away without ceremony. The sod was then neatly replaced, and spreading his blankets over the spot, Coronado had the least feverish sleep he had had in months.

The next morning Coronado took leave of the king of the Grand Quivíra and with bitter disappointment in his heart, only made bearable by the memory of one satisfactory deed, took the long trail back to Pecos.

He followed a straight route back, and in much less time than he had taken coming, he was back in Pecos.

The Indians of Pecos were having an old-time war dance when he arrived at the pueblo, for they had just had a brush with a raiding war party of Comanches. The Indians laid aside their war dance masks and received Coronado back to their town. They thought they had seen the last of him when he started away, led by the wily Turk, and now that he was back he was not in any manner welcome, but they made the best of things and entertained him. Coronado himself was not in a visiting mood, and the next day hurried on to his former headquarters at the pueblo of Sandía on the Rio Grande, and soon after that left for old Mexico with no more gold than he had had when he started north.

This was the greatest treasure hunt ever carried out in what is now the United States, and as long as the Indians lived at Pecos they never forgot the white men who lived in the little "iron houses."

Where Pecos once stood there is now only a large ruin, twenty-five miles east of Santa Fe, the capital of New Mexico. The last Indians deserted the pueblo in 1838, three hundred years after Coronado's time, and went to live with the Indians at Jemez pueblo, where their descendants still perform ceremonials brought from Pecos by their fathers.

ESTEVAN THE MAGNIFICENT

ESTEVAN THE MAGNIFICENT

THE story of Estevan, the negro, is partly recorded in various old Spanish chronicles, as well as to be encountered in the old lore of the Indians of Zuñi pueblo in New Mexico. The incidents of this ancient story happened only a few years after the discovery of America. Estevan, or Steven, as we would call him in English, experienced a most adventurous career, in which his destiny finally led him to one of the renowed seven cities of Cíbola of the great Zuñi nation. Steven was the first African negro to set foot among the pueblo Indians of the southwest, and the story of his adventures is as interesting and remarkable as that of any Spanish explorer or conquistador who ever ventured his life for renown or gold in the then unknown new world.

Steven began his career by being born on the west coast of Morocco in Africa. When he grew up he became a slave of the Spaniards, and we next hear of him as being with a great Spanish expedition that was exploring the Gulf of Mexico. After shipwreck and many hardships, he was cast, together with the Spanish survivors of the expedition, on the wild and swampy coast of Louisiana, just west of the mouth of the Mississippi River. Here they suffered such privation that they all perished except Steven and three of the Spaniards.

These four, with Cabeza de Baca, one of the Spaniards, as their leader, now started out to try to reach the Spanish settlements in Mexico by traveling overland afoot, and to do this they had to cross what is now Louisiana, Texas, New Mexico, and northern Mexico. This was in 1528, only thirty-six years after America was discovered, so that no white man had ever before traversed that part of the unknown country. It took them eight years to make the journey, suffering during that time innumerable hardships.

Most of this time they were captives of different tribes of the wild, roving Indians which they encountered one after the other. These Indians did not keep the four in captivity as slaves, but as great medicine men. Steven and the Spaniards always made the sign of the cross whenever they encountered Indians, to ward off harm to themselves. The sign of the cross to Indians is the symbol of the stars, so that when the sign of the cross was made, the Indians thought that the three white men and the black one meant to convey the information that they had come down from heaven. Hence the veneration in which they were held. Steven, as a great medicine man with divine powers, shared this veneration equally with the

Spaniards and forever after was spoiled, as far as being a good slave was concerned.

When the foot-weary wanderers finally reached the Spanish settlements in Mexico, in 1536, they caused a great sensation, and Cabeza de Baca afterward wrote the history of their wanderings.

Now the time spent by Steven among the Indians, perfecting his technique as a powerful medicine man, was a valuable education for him in the greatest adventure of his career.

In 1539 the viceroy of western Mexico decided to send a Spanish priest, Friar Marcos, into the country of the north on an exploring expedition, to see if there were any truth in the stories told by wandering Indians of great cities up there, filled with gold and other treasure. Of the seven cities of Cíbola the viceroy wanted information especially, for he had heard over and over again of their fabulous wealth. Cíbola we now know as Zuñi.

The viceroy chose Steven as interpreter and helper for Friar Marcos; for Steven's fame as a medicine man and conjurer, and his ability to impress the Indians, had spread all over those parts.

The little expedition set out on its long journey with Mexican Indians as guides and bearers. After they had traveled a part of the way together, Friar Marcos sent Steven on ahead to find out what he could of the country and report back to him. Steven was instructed that if he heard good news, he should send back a cross as large as his hand; if he heard better news, he was to send a cross as large as two hands; and if heard superlative news he was to send back a still larger cross. A few days later a cross came to the priest, by an Indian carrier, as large as a man.

Receiving this cross of good omen, Friar Marcos set out to overtake Steven, who had been told to await him at the place from which he should send the cross; but Steven had other plans. All during the journey he had been practising his rôle as medicine man among the wild Indians he had encountered along the way, and he had met with the most astonishing success. Indians prostrated themselves before him and felt blessed when they were even allowed to touch his garments. They freely gave him everything they had, even to their most prized possessions, so that he was bedecked with all the finery he could wear. Soon he had hundreds of adoring followers and a traveling harem of the most beautiful women.

All this adoration and deference went to his head and produced in him a state of grand pompousness, a state to which, as is well known, members of his race are prone when conditions are favorable. He assumed an overbearing air of the greatest authority over his abject followers, and they adored him all the more greatly for it. In his grand exaltation he quite forgot his duty to the priest; and instead of waiting for him as he had been commanded, he advanced in his triumphal march toward Zuñi, hastened by the wild tales his followers told him of the great wealth and the beautiful women to be had there for the taking; for these deluded believers in his divinity thought that he was irresistible, and that nothing could be denied him by any earthly power.

What could be more extravagant than the picture of this large, black, African negro, with his thick lips, flashing white teeth, crinkly beard and curly hair, advancing among Indians who later were considered the most treacherous and bloodthirsty on American soil, the Apaches of New Mexico—Indians who, it is said, would commit a murder or torture a captive with the most ingenious fiendishness; and instead of harming him, they adored him. They vied with one another in humbling themselves before him and felt themselves amply rewarded if he but glanced in their direction. No god could command such reverence and subservience as they bestowed on him. No white man was ever so received by Indians. The only reason accounting for it is that Steven's recent emergence from savagery gave him an intuitive knowledge of the power which a personal assumption of supreme self-confidence, exhibiting itself in a condescending arrogance and coupled with a powerful personality, has on the primitive mind.

Whereas a civilized white man would have been disgusted and annoyed at many of these Indians' exuberant acts of adulation and worship, this amazing negro encouraged them in their extravagances. The women clamored for his favors. The men cleared the way before him. They danced and leaped in front of him. They shouted to the skies that this was the greatest medicine man in the world. They yelled their adulation of him, and Steven found it all very good and satisfying to his vanity.

Finally the wild horde arrived at Zuñi. At the head of the mob was the pompous and grandiose Steven, who by now, on account of the great homage paid him, had come to believe in his own greatness.

As Steven stood before the entrance to Zuñi he was an impressive spectacle. On his head was a head-dress of gorgeous parrot feathers; around his neck were hung innumerable strands of turquoise and wampum; from his shoulders hung a mantle woven of brilliantly colored bird feathers, and on his ankles and wrists were bright, tinkly bells of copper. In his hand he carried the symbol of the medicine man as he had come to know it, a large, hollow gourd rattle with a white and red feather tied to it, and on his face was an expression of arrogant self confidence absolutely supreme.

Steven knocked at the gate of the pueblo and called loudly for admittance. The chief men of the pueblo and the cacique, or high priest, came to look Steven over and demanded of him what he wanted. Steven was not small in his demands. He drew himself up in his most haughty and over-bearing manner and told the Zuñis that he wanted admittance to the pueblo immediately, and that he also wanted the best that the pueblo afforded for himself and followers. He also told the Zuñis, with no show of false modesty, that he was the greatest medicine man in the world and had un-limited powers as a conjurer.

Now these Zuñis were of a different caliber from any Indians that Steven had ever before en-countered. They were civilized, intelligent, and canny, and were not in the habit of taking the word of a perfect stranger as to his worth. They scrutinized Steven deliberately and with care, and their expressions were those of unmistakable dis-approval. They told Steven sourly that the gourd he carried was the symbol of the medicine men of the wild Indians, their enemies, and that the bells he wore were not in the style of a strictly high-class medicine man, and that as far as they could see he was just another Mexican Indian, though somewhat blacker than the others. They also refused with definite finality to accept him or allow him in the pueblo.

Steven's self-assurance was somewhat abated at this. It was the first time that he had encountered Indians as civilized and incredulous as these. Nevertheless, backed by his followers, he tried to bluster his way into the pueblo and to bulldoze the Zuñis into accepting him at his own estimation.

The result of this was immediate battle. The Zuñi warriors fell on him and his gullible followers in a business-like way and made quick work of them. Many of Steven's worshipers were slain by the Zuñis. Others, seeing the hopelessness of the situation, abandoned the battle and ran away. A few were captured, along with all the loot that Steven had brought.

As for Steven, the Zuñis carefully plucked him of all his gay feathers and gaudy finery and lodged him in a small, dark strong room where he was no longer "the greatest medicine man in the world," but just a plain, ordinary, scared to death negro, without a friend in sight.

The Zuñis now proceeded to give the captives they had taken with Steven the third degree; and these captives, seeing that all his glory was departed from him and that Steven's medicine was powerless to help him in his present situation, shamelessly betrayed and abandoned their former god, and in order to gain favor with their captors falsely accused Steven of having killed women who displeased him, and said that he had come to Zuñi to take all the beautiful women there. The Zuñis were highly incensed at this, for they cherish their women and have a very high regard for them.

The Zuñis then proceeded to question Steven; and since they have always been past masters in applying the third degree, they were not long in wringing from the now thoroughly frightened negro all there was to know. That finished, they proceeded to knock Steven on the head; and then threw his naked body over the wall. An escaping captive saw it there that night and carried word of the tragedy back to the Spanish priest.

Thus came to an end, at the pueblo of Zuñi, the career of the greatest tragi-comedy figure that ever came in contact with pueblo Indians of the southwest.

PARROT FEATHERS

ONE afternoon I sat on the edge of the roof of a kiva or ceremonial room at the old Hopi pueblo of Walpi. It was the kiva nearest the west end of the mesa and there was a fine view of the desert to the southward. With me sat a Hopi friend, Morning Cloud, who was well versed in the old legends of the Hopis. As we looked off toward the rim of the desert I asked Morning Cloud where the Hopis came from, and how they happened to come to Walpi.

"Well," he said, "I only know the story as it has been told by the old men from the time long ago, but I will tell it as I have heard it, and I believe it is true."

* * * * *

Different clans of the Hopis came from different places. Some of them came from the north, some from the west and some from the great river in the east, but we, the first and oldest Hopis, came from the south. Many hundreds of years ago we lived in the great kingdom of Montezuma in old Mexico. We lived in the country near the great western sea and had a beautiful pueblo there. We raised much corn and cotton and wove very beautiful cloth, which we traded to Montezuma, of which to make clothing and blankets. For a long time we lived very happily there in Mexico, but finally the first great Montezuma died and his son became Montezuma in his place. This second Montezuma was very different from his father, and did not treat the people in the same kind way. The first great Montezuma was guided by and helped by the Great Spirit, but his son became a wizard and served the Evil One. He made soldiers or slaves of all the people, and all the prisoners he took in war he killed on the altar of the God of War. We Hopis were peaceful people and did not want to fight, so he made slaves of all of us, and made us weave cloth all the time for himself and his soldiers, and we became very unhappy, but we never stopped worshiping the Great Spirit.

At last our cacique asked the Great Spirit to help us in our trouble, and in response to the prayers he sent his sacred parrot to aid us. The parrot flew down out of the sky and alighted on the top rung of our ceremonial kiva ladder and talked to us. He told us that he had been sent to us by the Great Spirit, to lead us out of the kingdom of the wicked Montezuma to a new home far distant in the northland, where the soldiers of Montezuma could not follow us and where we could live in freedom and safety, and that there the Great Spirit would watch over us always.

The parrot said that he would fly ahead of us and show us the road that we should take to the new home that had been chosen for us. The parrot also told us to prepare all the food that we could carry to eat on the journey, and when this was done the parrot flew to the northward and all of us followed after him.

We traveled in this way for a very long distance. After many weeks, we were so weary we could follow no longer and our food was also nearly gone. Then the parrot alighted and commanded us to build a pueblo, make fields, and plant corn, and rest until we were strong and had plenty of food, so that we could continue our voyage. We obeyed, and after we had lived there a few years the parrot appeared again and told us to again gather food and prepare to take up our journey to the northward. So in a short time we had left this pueblo behind and were following the parrot once more.

Again we traveled a long distance to the northward, until our food was nearly all gone and we were worn out with the traveling, and so now the parrot alighted and told us to do as we did before. So we built another pueblo and planted more fields and raised more corn to live on. We rested in this place for many years, until the parrot again appeared and told us to follow as we did before. This same thing happened a great many times. We would travel a long way and would then have to stop and build a pueblo and raise more corn and rest, and then the parrot would appear and we would follow him again to the northward. The ruins of these old pueblos can still be seen all the way from here to Mexico. We built our largest pueblo and stayed the longest time at a place we called Homolobi on the Little Colorado River, not far from where Holbrook now stands.

At last after many years we arrived at this high rocky mesa. Here there was a cave that was like a kiva, and a pole ladder reached out of the top of the cave. The parrot alighted on the top of this ladder and told us that this was to be our home always from then on, and that now he must return to the Great Spirit who had sent him, but before going he told us that we must always keep our name Hopi-to, which means peaceful people. He also told us always to receive and treat well all people who came to us for help, or those who were fleeing from whoever were trying to enslave them. Then the parrot left us and flew straight up into the sky and disappeared.

We have followed the parrot's advice and have always been the peaceful Hopi people, and many other people have come from far off places to live with us. The last ones to come were people from the great river in the east. These people came here over two hundred years ago and live at Hano, and they came here to escape the Spaniards, who were trying to make slaves of them.

This kiva on which we now sit is built over the cave where the parrot rested and talked to us after leading us here. For many years we kept a wooden parrot fastened to the top of this ladder. At last it fell into pieces, so now we wear parrot feathers on our heads when we give our most sacred dances, to let the Great Spirit know that we have not forgotten his kindness to us by sending his sacred parrot to lead us out of our slavery in the kingdom of Montezuma to our home here.

MONTEZUMA

THE TWELVE VIRGINS OF PECOS

MONTEZUMA

ALL primitive peoples recognize the benefits conferred on them by the sun and are therefore, in the beginning, more or less sun worshipers. As time goes on, they personify the sun and make of this personage a great culture hero, and weave about him and his exploits many stories which later become legends. The Pueblo Indians of New Mexico have their great sun hero, but the myth of this culture hero varies somewhat in the different pueblos. The following myth I received from a Tewa Indian of one of the upper Rio Grande pueblos, and I have made a free translation of what he told me. It is a myth that has gradually evolved. A part of it is very old and pagan; other parts, through Mexican influence, have been added within the past hundred years or so, and there can also be detected in it some elements of missionary teaching.

Pose Ueve, whose name means "He who scatters the mists in the morning," was born in the large pueblo of Pose Uingge, which is now a large prehistoric ruin near the hot springs twenty miles north of the present Tewa pueblo of San Juan. "Pose Ueve," my Indian informant told me naïvely, "was born without a father like the

Christian Jesus, which perhaps made him very unusual."

At any rate, he was very unusual for a normal Indian boy. He never played with the other children of the pueblo nor helped his mother, who was very poor, with the work. He went unkempt and spent most of his time wandering through the woods and over the mountains. He made friends of all the wild animals and birds, and talked with them. Often he was heard talking as with invisible beings, and on account of all these things the pueblo considered him a simpleton, and scorned him as one of no account.

When Pose Ueve was nearly grown the cacique, the high priest of the pueblo and practically its ruler, died without having appointed his successor, so a new cacique had to be chosen by lot. Every man in the pueblo had to take part in the lottery, and in this way the choice chanced to fall to Pose Ueve. The older and more intelligent men of the pueblo were horrified at this state of affairs which chance had brought about and which they considered a disaster, while the others considered it a great joke.

Pose Ueve, however, took his election very seriously and from that moment was a different man. His mother and grandmother made him the most beautiful clothes of which they were capable and ornamented them with the sky-colored turquoise. When Pose Ueve had washed himself and arranged his hair properly, and arrayed himself in his new clothes, everyone was amazed at his handsome appearance and could not believe he was the same Pose Ueve they had always seen so ragged and unkempt.

As cacique, Pose Ueve did not disappoint the people in other things. He knew where all the different kinds of game were to be found and he could always tell the hunters where to hunt, so that the people had plenty of meat. Also he had the power to call the clouds at any time to bring the rain, so that there was never any fear of drought, and there was always abundance of corn in the pueblo. No raiding Apaches nor Navajos could surprise the pueblo, because Pose Ueve always knew when they were near and had his warriors ready to drive them away.

But in spite of the fact that Pose Ueve was such an efficient cacique, his present position had its handicaps. Some of the people could not forget his former state. Those who had looked down on Pose Ueve and were now being surpassed by him would not show the respect to their cacique that his exalted office demanded. Also he was accused by the conservative old men of the pueblo of being a radical, and of not following in the ways of the ancients. All this angered Pose Ueve so greatly that he suddenly disappeared for all time from the pueblo of Pose Uingge.

Later he appeared at the pueblo of Pecos, far to the southeast of Pose Uingge. Here he became cacique and a great ruler, and soon Pecos, from being a small and obscure pueblo, became the greatest and most powerful pueblo in all of New Mexico. People came there from everywhere and joined the pueblo on account of the prosperity brought to it by its wise ruler, who, on coming to Pecos, had assumed the name of Montezuma, and by the name of Montezuma he was known from then on.

The reason for Montezuma's great success as a ruler and cacique was that he permitted himself to be guided in all that he did by the Great Spirit. Soon after Montezuma came to Pecos, the Great Spirit revealed to him that he should marry the youngest daughter of the cacique of the pueblo of Zuñi; so in obedience to the dictates of the Great Spirit he sent an embassy to Zuñi to request this girl, whose name was Malinche, as his bride. The cacique of Zuñi was pleased that such a powerful ruler as Montezuma desired his daughter as wife and gladly gave his consent to the marriage. Malinche then went to Pecos with the ambassadors and became Montezuma's queen.

Montezuma and Malinche then ruled their people in such an enlightened manner that the radical and progressive elements of the different pueblos, who were discontented with the old conservative ways of their own people, flocked to them, and soon there was not sufficient room for them all at Pecos, so Montezuma decided to found other pueblos with the overflow of these people.

To assist him the Great Spirit sent his sacred eagle to guide Montezuma in this work. The eagle flew ahead of Montezuma and his people, and wherever the eagle alighted a pueblo was built. In this way nearly all of the later pueblos in New Mexico were built, and they were populated by the many people who followed Montezuma. Always Montezuma traveled to the southward, and one day after he had traveled a long distance the eagle seized a serpent in his beak and alighted on a cactus plant. This was the sign long awaited by Montezuma, and at this place he stopped and built his capital, where Mexico City now stands, and as his insignia he adopted the sacred eagle sitting on a cactus plant, holding a serpent in its beak.

With his new city as a capital, Montezuma established a great kingdom over which he and Malinche ruled. Later they became rulers over the great country of the Aztecs; but always they recognized with gratitude the help of the Great

Spirit in their affairs. The Evil One often tried to tempt them to serve him. He promised them power over the whole world if they would worship him, but they never allowed themselves to be shaken in their allegiance to their great benefactor.

To this day, many of the Indian pueblos in New Mexico enact each year a dance drama which they call "Matachina," in which Montezuma and Malinche are the hero and the heroine, and the Evil One is the villain who tempts them, but who is never quite able to triumph over them. In this dance Malinche always carries a three-pronged wand, representing the Trinity.

Also, because of this legend in which Montezuma always moves to the southward, no pueblo Indians ever move their ceremonial plaza to the northward, for fear of incurring the displeasure of the Great Spirit and of all the pueblos. San Ildefonso alone has had the temerity to attempt this. Many years ago they moved their plaza to the northward, but misfortunes and deaths so multiplied among them that they are again performing their ceremonial dances in the ancient south plaza, and since then their prosperity has increased.

* * * * *

THE TWELVE VIRGINS OF PECOS

THIS story of the twelve virgins of Pecos was told me by a son of the last living Pecos Indian, as follows:

Montezuma, before leaving Pecos, lighted a sacred fire on the Sun Altar and commanded that this fire must be fed and kept burning continuously, day and night, by twelve virgin daughters of the head men of the pueblo, and he told the head men that as long as this fire was kept burning Pecos would prosper, and that some time he himself would return and again rule over the pueblo.

This sacred fire was kept alive and ceremonies were held yearly in honor of Montezuma for many centuries. But one night the twelve virgins, made drowsy by the heat of the fire, fell asleep, and the sacred flame died and the altar became cold.

For their negligence the virgins were punished, disgraced and made outcasts, but from that time the prosperity of the pueblo quickly diminished, and the population declined so much that the head men of Pecos came to the conclusion that the pueblo was accursed because the sacred fire had gone out, and decided to abandon Pecos and go and live with their kinsmen at Jemez, a pueblo which Montezuma had founded with the overflow of population from Pecos, and where yearly their descendants still perform some of the ceremonies brought from the home of their fathers.

The last Pecos Indians deserted their pueblo in 1838, and the disintegrating ruin of this once large Indian community, which lies twenty-five miles east of Santa Fe, is now a great mine from which Dr. Kidder, the archaeologist, brings forth evidences of the past greatness of this once numerous people.